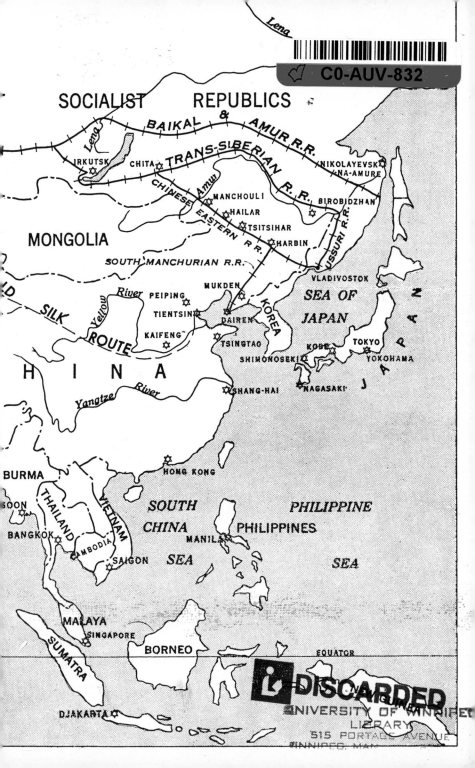

SOCIALIST   REPUBLICS

BAIKAL & AMUR R.R.

Lena

TRANS-SIBERIAN R.R.

IRKUTSK   CHITA

NIKOLAYEVSK NA-AMURE

CHINESE EASTERN R.R.   Amur   MANCHOULI   BIROBIDZHAN

HAILAR

TSITSIHAR

MONGOLIA

SOUTH MANCHURIAN R.R.   HARBIN

USSURI R.R.

VLADIVOSTOK

Yellow River   PEIPING   MUKDEN

SILK   TIENTSIN   DAIREN   KOREA   SEA OF JAPAN

ROUTE   KAIFENG

TSINGTAO   KOBE   TOKYO

H I N A   SHIMONOSEKI   YOKOHAMA

Yangtze River   SHANG-HAI   NAGASAKI   J A P A N

HONG KONG

BURMA   SOUTH   PHILIPPINE

SOON   THAILAND   VIETNAM   CHINA   PHILIPPINES

BANGKOK   CAMBODIA   SEA   MANILA   SEA

SAIGON

MALAYA   SINGAPORE

SUMATRA   BORNEO   EQUATOR

DJAKARTA

WANDERERS AND SETTLERS IN THE FAR EAST

WANDERERS AND SETTLERS
IN THE FAR EAST

*A Century of Jewish Life
in China and Japan*

By

HERMAN DICKER

TWAYNE PUBLISHERS, INC.
NEW YORK

MANUFACTURED IN THE UNITED STATES OF AMERICA

TYPOGRAPHY BY BARDU LINOTYPING SERVICE INC., NEW YORK

TO EILEEN, MY DEVOTED WIFE

INTRODUCTION

THE STORY told in this book, in a sense obscure and yet of vital importance to Jewish history, had its genesis in my assignment to Japan in 1956. Although I was not the first United States Army chaplain to serve in Japan, it later developed that I was destined to be the last of a procession of uniformed rabbinical emissaries from the United States. Thus, I fell heir to the accumulated good will of my predecessors. At the same time, I also inherited their responsibilities—freely assumed—toward the civilian Jewish population of Tokyo.

I deeply appreciated the good will and I welcomed the opportunity to serve those Jews in Tokyo who were not in uniform. Over the years, all the Jewish chaplains, indeed, all chaplains regardless of faith or creed, had done all within their power and ability to aid dislocated men, women and children in their brave efforts to reestablish their lives in faraway places following the violence and conflagration of World War II.

Since 1953, the hub of Jewish life in Japan was to be found in the Jewish Community Center of Tokyo. Curiously, the Center was not easy to find or to enjoy. One had to fight with taxi drivers and struggle with street signs, in Japanese, of course, to locate it for it was hidden behind a wall in a residential section of the city, called Shibuya. But the effort to find the Center itself, difficult on its own, was only part of the problem. I do not mean that the doors were barred to those who went to

7

the trouble to find it. On the contrary, military personnel and civilian transients, somehow or other, managed to discover the Center and take advantage of its facilities. What was extremely complicated was to get "inside" the hearts and minds of the Jewish families that belonged to the Center. There were about one hundred such families and to win their hearts was the greater challenge.

I should begin by stating, at the very outset, that the edifice itself was impressive and beautiful. The synagogue was newly added to a lovely Japanese mansion and the entire Center provided a meeting place for Jews from all parts of the world. The Center permitted Jews from China and Russia and Europe and the Near East, as well as soldiers from the United States, to come together, to learn a little about one another. It afforded Jews the opportunity to make contact, to begin to understand one another. Oddly enough, there were Japanese who, for reasons of their own, attended our services. So it was that Jews had a unique experience in faraway Japan: they not only made the acquaintance of fellow Jews from obscure and hidden corners of the world: they also were able to learn something about the Japanese in their midst.

As a Jewish chaplain serving in the United States Army, I was especially fortunate in having the use of this house of worship. Its central location, its excellent social and kitchen facilities, made it a welcome haven for weary soldiers from Japan and Korea who were seeking relaxation and forgetfulness. Still, it was not easy to relax in Japan for soldiers of diverse backgrounds. There were differences in language, in customs, in interests, in outlook on life. Add to this the obvious fact that the Jewish families belonging to the Center also came from sharply different backgrounds—plus the crowded, limited space in the Center—and you are faced with a job which requires more than the usual patience a chaplain needs for a unit of American troops from, say, New York.

Nevertheless, it always is a challenge to meet people on their own grounds, to attempt to probe their souls, to demonstrate to them that we really care about them and the enormous problems they face, problems thrust upon them from the outside, under harsh circumstances. As we took the time to interest ourselves in them, the Jewish families of the Center gradually warmed to us. They opened their hearts and those who had homes of their own invited us to visit with them.

It was natural, under these conditions, that many questions came to mind and cried for answers. What was the background of these resident Jews and what fate had brought them to this remote corner of the earth?

My own personal history had given me some of the answers. I, too, had lived in many lands, and not by my own free choice. Hungary . . . Germany . . . Switzerland . . . Palestine and the United States had been my major stopping points before World War II. Then, the United States Army had called upon me in the war against Nazi tyranny in Europe. I had shared the hardships of the front-line soldier and in the triumphs of breaking down the walls of the concentration camps in Germany. I had had the privilege of helping displaced persons of Europe to get back on their feet, and I had helped many of them by escorting them to the shores of the new State of Israel.

Thus, when I met the handful of Jews in the Far East, I could approach them, in a sense, as a fellow Jew who understood their wanderings and their hopes, for I had shared their anguish and had been, in the recent past, a stranger myself in a world I never made.

There was, however, an additional element of flavor in their stories, for they had lived in the Orient, and it was precisely this Oriental background that was entirely new to me. I was intrigued, and wanted to learn more about the Orient and about them. I started probing, gently, into their personal histories prior to their arrival in Japan. At first, my questions were met with suspicion. I understood this reaction, for all too often in their lives they had become the victims of investigators and questioners in uniform. But then I told them of my intention to record their experiences and their lives in Manchuria and China before they came to Japan. Slowly, their reluctance to share their experiences turned to full cooperation. They realized that their experiences deserved a place in Jewish history and, if not gathered at this time, would be swept away by the swift current of human events.

It was in this fashion that we started tracing their stories, from Tokyo to Shanghai and from there to Harbin—to mention only a few of the most important Jewish settlements in the Far East.

Inextricably woven into every story was encounter after encounter with the Japanese. I realized at this point that one could not appreciate the full picture unless the Japanese reaction to these Jews was understood. I found myself asking many questions of Japanese, wondering how they felt about the Jews in their midst. It was evident to me that talking to a Japanese in the 1950's could not offer a proper perspective into the events of the 1930's or 1940's. Moreover, I was not interested in excuses over past behavior or criticisms of past events. My aim was to obtain the facts or, if I possibly could, official documents of the period under investigation.

Fortunately, all documents relating to Jews in Japan during World War II had not all been destroyed. There still existed, I discovered, five voluminous but uncatalogued volumes of material on Jewish matters in the archives of the Japanese Foreign Office, as well as some papers in private hands. As soon as I learned of the existence of these papers, I sought, and received, full cooperation from the Japanese. Friendly staff sections lent me their best Japanese interpreters and there commenced a feverish job of copying, translating and evaluating. Japanese authorities were extraordinarily helpful, even to the degree that my Japanese co-workers and I were served tea as we worked with dusty files in the small, crowded research room of the Foreign Office. Professor Masayuki Kobayashi of Waseda University and my own efficient secretary, Miss Masae Kawahara, I must add, gave me inestimable aid and comfort in the heavy task I had undertaken.

In all fairness, I should mention many more names of friends whose support has made this enterprise possible. But memory and space are too limited to do all of them justice. I hope they will forgive and derive satisfaction from seeing the story in print. However one I cannot overlook. He is Harold U. Ribalow, whose literary talent and devotion to the subject breathed life into my research and personal investigation as reported in the following pages. I feel that this material, valuable in itself, has special importance because it is basic, original, hitherto unknown to the historians of World War II and, particularly, to the Jewish historians. While it is true that Jewish history is rich in documentation and in human interest, it is equally true that much of it has been lost to our generation and to future generations because of the loss of material and, at times, the indifference of the historian.

The Jews in the Far East during World War II survived not only as human beings under duress, but as aware, proud Jews. Theirs is a most remarkable and unusual story. I hope that it is told adequately in these pages.

CONTENTS

WANDERERS AND SETTLERS IN THE FAR EAST

CHAPTER I

MANCHURIA

THE STORY OF JEWISH SETTLEMENT in the Far East begins in
Manchuria. In order to understand and trace Jewish life in this
distant part of the world, it is necessary, first, that Manchuria
itself be placed in geographical and historical focus. Otherwise,
the picture may be fuzzy rather than clear.

Manchuria itself has a total area of 503,254 square miles.
Always considered an integral part of China—until it was occupied by the Japanese in 1931—Manchuria is largely Chinese in
population. According to the first official census, taken in 1940,
there were about 42,000,000 Chinese in the area; 900,000 Japanese; 1,200,000 Koreans and 65,000 men, women and children
from other lands. The total population was approximately
44,000,000.

Manchuria is separated from Siberia in the north by the
Amur River. On the western side, Manchuria is separated from
Mongolia by mountain ranges. In the east, Manchuria is divided
from the Russian province of Ussuri by the Ussuri River. In
the southwest section, Manchuria is parted from Korea by the
Tumen and Yalu Rivers. The Great Wall in the southwest sepa-
rates the country from Hopei, which is a province of North
China.

It is a land with many mountains, lakes and rivers—and much

17

beauty as well. The Sungari River plays a key role in Manchuria's daily life, for much of the land's cultivated area is drained and watered by the Sungari and its tributaries.

Until the Japanese occupation in 1931, Manchuria was divided into three provinces, Liaoning, Kirin and Heilung Kang—which is why the Chinese name for Manchuria was "Tung San Sheng," meaning "Three Eastern Provinces." The efficient Japanese, eager to alter and control along their own lines, divided the three provinces into fourteen, thus attempting to bring greater efficiency to their administration of the territory.

As Japanese influence increased, the Russian population declined steadily. In 1931, there were 140,000 Russians in Manchuria, but when the Chinese Eastern Railway was sold to the Japanese in 1935, some 20,000 railway employees left the country. By 1940, the Russian community was at its greatest peak in Harbin. About 27,000 White Russians made their home there.

Manchuria was caught in a squeeze between Japanese and Russian expansion. As early as 1847, the Russians had begun to eye the vast area of Manchuria and to add up the value of its enormous natural resources. The Russians had first become acquainted with Manchuria when Count Muraviev was appointed Viceroy of Eastern Siberia in 1847. A Russian naval force had occupied Vladivostok in 1860 and once again Manchuria was placed in the forefront of Russian expansionist plans.

Following the conclusion of the Sino-Japanese War in 1895, the Liaotung Peninsula, which was the southern portion of Fengtien Province, was ceded to Japan. However, representations on the part of Russia, Germany and France induced the Japanese to accept money in lieu of this territory, which eventually was leased to Russia in 1898.

It was during this same year that Russia acquired the right to construct a railway from Harbin to Port Arthur. This move indicated progress for the Russians who, two years earlier, had secured a similar right to build a railroad line from Manchouli in the west to the eastern Ussuri border. These two lines later became known as the Chinese Eastern Railway.

With the outbreak of the famous Boxer Rebellion, Manchuria was occupied by the Russians. Two years later, and after much negotiation, the Russians agreed to remove their troops—within eighteen months. Conflicting interests between Russia and Japan—too complex to enter into in this account which, after all, must deal with such matters in comparatively cursory fashion—led to the Russo-Japanese War, which ended in victory for the Japanese. It also resulted in the Treaty of Portsmouth in 1905, in which American President Theodore Roosevelt played a major role.

As a result of their victory, the Japanese won the territory of Kwantung and all rights and privileges relating to the Chinese Eastern Railway, south of Changchun. The Russians pledged to restore Manchuria to China.

Nearly twenty years later, in 1924, Chinese and Russian authorities found themselves in deep conflict over the operation of the railroad. In their own defense, the Russians occupied North Manchuria in reply to the aggressive policies of Marshal Chang Tso-lin, the military dictator of the country. By the time 1931 rolled around, Russian influence was strong in Outer Mongolia. Simultaneously, China's nationalistic spirit waxed stronger and it was apparent that the Chinese wished to recover what she considered to be her rights in Manchuria. Japan, meanwhile, felt that her "special position" was being threatened and in 1931 an incident—an explosion near the railway at Mukden—led to the long, tedious and terrible war between China and Japan.

Many books have been written about this war and this account will not in any way attempt to compete with the complete histories which fill library shelves all over the world. However, mention must be made of this background if the reader is to understand, a bit further along in this narrative, the situation of the Jewish people in this part of the world while earthshaking and enormous events were taking place.

It is sufficient for the purposes of this narrative to point out that while the Chinese–Japanese war was of long duration and, indeed, continued during World War II, the immediate result was that Japan occupied the entire territory of Manchuria and proclaimed the state of Manchukuo. Later on, of course, the League of Nations found that Manchukuo was a Japanese instrumentality and was by no means an independent state. In 1935, the Chinese Eastern Railway was transferred from the Russians to the Japanese for the sum of 170,000,000 yen. But this did not assure peace between the two nations. There were constant border disputes between Soviet and Manchurian authorities—all of which added to the tensions existing within the State.

The political and social tensions of Manchuria grew most intense in 1945, when Soviet Russia entered the war against Japan on August 8, 1945, only six days before the Japanese surrendered, following the dropping of the A-bomb on Hiroshima and Nagasaki. Taking advantage of their conquering position, the Russians occupied all of Manchuria. In 1946, the Russians evacuated the territory, after having stripped the northeastern sector of all its industrial equipment.

On April 25, 1946, Communist Chinese troops, now in control of China, captured Harbin. As of this date, all of Manchuria is held by and administered by the Chinese Communists.

It is easy to fathom why both the Soviet Union and Japan were so deeply interested in Manchuria, for the area is extraordinarily fertile and contains many rich resources. Manchuria is the third largest producer of soya beans, standing behind China and the United States. Some sixty per cent of the entire population is engaged in agriculture, with about eighty per cent of the people of Manchuria living on farms. Because the summers are comparatively brief, only those crops are grown which can mature quickly. This is the reason why eighty-five per cent of the total area under cultivation is restricted to soya and other beans. Statistics available for the period of the 1930's reveal that the average annual production of soya beans comes to 4,000,000 tons, which is the equivalent of 146,000,000 bushels. China produces 225,000,000 bushels and the United States 210,000,000.

The Manchurians also produce millet, maize, wheat and rice, as well as cotton, hemp, flax, tobacco and ground nuts. In addition to these useful crops, Manchuria boasts of a rich timber industry, as well as fisheries and minerals. The Japanese, with their ever-growing population on their small islands, were especially eager to exploit the natural resources of Manchuria, in view of their own lack of these natural riches. It was particularly simple to mine Manchuria's coal, which is bituminous and lies in thick beds close to the surface of the earth. Iron and coal, being readily available, were also useful for the Japanese iron and steel industries.

Harbin

The city of Harbin, which already has cropped up in this narrative and will continue to play a major role in the story of Jewish settlement in the Far East, was the core of the Russian community in Manchuria. It symbolized the deep penetration of Russia into China. Of utmost importance to the Russians was the Chinese Eastern Railway which, to all intents and purposes, was in Russian territory. Russia had complete rights and jurisdiction in the area in which the railway ran. The railway's main line, with a depth of ten miles on either side, extended from Manchouli to Vladivostok, by way of Harbin. Work on the road commenced in 1898 and the line was completed in 1901, covering Manchuria's entire distance of 925 miles. A secondary line was built from Harbin to Port Arthur, which was completed in 1903 and covered 637 miles. The southern sector of the railway was established in 1905 by the Japanese.

In the short span of one generation, from 1900 to 1930, Harbin bloomed from a sleepy village of a thousand or so people into a busy metropolis of 300,000. Because it was established by the Russians, it was more European than Chinese in spirit and tempo.

The Jewish residents of Harbin played an important role in developing and building this city, which was a pioneering Russian effort in this part of the world. Before the Japanese moved in, in 1932, the Jewish population alone expanded from 1,500 (in 1910) to 13,000 (in 1930). Soon after 1930, when the Japanese arrived, the city went into an economic decline, due to the commercial restrictions placed upon businessmen of foreign descent.

The Jews had come to Manchuria and to Harbin from European and Siberian Russia as early as 1898. The story is told that the Jews were permitted to emigrate to the area in order to speed up and develop trade in Manchuria. It was thanks to the intervention of Prince Vladimir Kokovtzeff, the Russian Finance Minister from 1904 to 1914, that Jews were welcomed to Manchuria. One group of settlers arrived in 1904 to serve as contractors for the army of the Russian Czar. A few hundred more Jews, who had served as soldiers in the Russian army, settled in Harbin. The major factor in swelling the Jewish population was the Russian Revolution, which was fought from 1917 to 1920. In those years thousands of Jews found their way to Harbin, bringing the Jewish population to more than 10,000.

In 1935, the Japan Chamber of Commerce and Industry published a directory which helps to illuminate the economic situation of the Jews in the city. The book was entitled *A Directory of White Russian Jews in North Manchuria*. It lists a total of

112 establishments run by Jews. Four of these firms were founded before 1910, sixteen before 1920, seventy-one before 1930 and twenty-one prior to 1935. These statistics indicate most clearly that the greatest economic expansion occurred between the end of World War I and the Japanese occupation in 1931.

Most of the Jews were in the export-import business, dealing in textiles, furs, dry goods, lumber, grain and general merchandising. Among the pioneers who helped develop the city of Harbin were the Bonner, Kabalkin, Patushinsky, Skidelsky and Soskin families. S. L. Skidelsky had been decorated by the Chinese Government for his relief efforts on behalf of hundreds of people affected by the famine in China in 1921.

There also were two Jewish banks—the Far Eastern Jewish Bank of Commerce, established in 1921, and the Jewish People's Bank, founded in 1935. The Jewish People's Bank still functions under the Chinese Communists. Albert Parry, a specialist in Russian and Far Eastern affairs, reported that on the eve of the Japanese occupation, the Japanese owned or controlled only eight per cent of Harbin's private industries. Chinese businessmen and industrialists owned fifty-eight per cent and Russian (non-Soviet) and Russian-Jewish interests, owned thirty-three per cent of the private businesses. But by 1934, only two years after the Japanese occupation, the Japanese held all the shipbuilding enterprises in the city as well as many of the soya bean and flour mills. They also reorganized the grain exchange, placing it under their control. As a result of this reorganization, Kabalkin was forced to resign as president of the Stock Exchange Committee. By 1939, Japanese capital owned twelve per cent of all of the most significant business firms and handled some thirty per cent of Harbin's entire trade.

It is thus easy to comprehend why the Jewish population dwindled from 13,000 to 5,000 in the decade from 1929 to 1939.

Cultural Life in Harbin

Like Jews everywhere, the Jews of Harbin organized an intensive cultural life in their city. Their imagination, hard work and idealism led the Harbin Jews to create a center to which all the other scattered Manchurian-Jewish communities were able to turn.

Harbin Jewry established, rapidly and solidly, a synagogue, a Talmud Torah, a cheder, an old age home and a cemetery. The Talmud Torah was begun in 1910 and completed four years later. But the Jews failed in their attempt to convert the Talmud Torah into a Jewish high school, with Russian as the basic language.

Yiddish was the spoken tongue of the first generation of settlers, except for those who had arrived from Siberia. Siberian Jewry was small in 1914. There were only 35,000 Jews out of a total population of 10,000,000. Originally the Jews in the area had been deported to Siberia as "criminals" or had come there as ex-soldiers. Yet once the Jews had settled in Siberia and had served their "term," they enjoyed almost full civil rights and attained a level of economic security much higher than that enjoyed by their fellow Jews in European Russia.

The Siberian Jews, of course, spoke Russian, which was the native tongue of Harbin's second generation of Jews. One of the most colorful personalities in Harbin—and in its development—was E. Dobisoff, who served as chief of the municipal services. Dobisoff was a scrupulously honest leader who died penniless in 1918.

The community itself was highly organized and called itself the Harbin Hebrew Association. Its two outstanding leaders were Rabbi Aron Moshe Kiseleff and Dr. Abraham Kaufman. In close friendship and complete harmony, these two men managed the affairs of the Harbin community. Later, in turbulent and difficult times, they also gave guidance to other Jewish communities in the Far East.

Rabbi Kiseleff was a great Talmudic scholar who first came to Harbin when he was in his forties. He was born in Sores, Russia, in 1866 and as a child excelled in Jewish studies. He soon became known as the Vietker Ilui (wonder child), taking his name from the Yeshiva he attended as a youth. At sixteen, he transferred to the Yeshiva of Minsk and, two years later, moved over to the Talmudic Center of Volozhin, where he studied with the famed Rabbi Chaim Soloveitchik. Rabbi Soloveitchik had many world-renowned students who became great rabbis on their own. One of them was the late Rabbi Abraham Isaac Kuk, the Chief Rabbi of Israel.

Rabbi Kiseleff was ordained by Rabbi Chaim Ozer Grodzenski and then served as the rabbi of Borisoff from 1900 to 1913. In his final year at Borisoff, in 1913, Rabbi Kiseleff was called to Harbin and he accepted the post as spiritual head there at the gentle urging of the Lubavitcher Rebbe.

Within a short period of time, Rabbi Kiseleff won the love and admiration of the entire community and achieved a great deal in raising the spiritual level of this remote Jewish congregation. It was, therefore, fitting that in 1937 he was elected, unanimously, as Chief Rabbi by the General Conference of the Far Eastern Jewish Communities.

During the last years of his life, Rabbi Kiseleff was placed under heavy pressure by the local authorities; nevertheless, he continued to do all within his power to aid his fellow Jews. It was due to his prestige and qualities of leadership that the communal institutions continued to function effectively until his death, at the age of eighty-three, in 1949.

In 1915, when there was a heavy influx of refugees from Russia, Rabbi Kiseleff worked tirelessly on their behalf in the face of official disapproval. The disapproval was more than cursory or verbal, for the rabbi was sentenced to a three-month prison term for his "illegal" work.

He survived, of course, and continued his literary and scholarly labors. In 1931, he published *Nationalism and Judaism*, a Russian-language volume of sermons and lectures on the significance of Judaism. Rabbi Kiseleff hoped that the volume would point up to the youths of the community the values of their Jewish heritage.

Rabbi Kiseleff enjoyed the friendship of all the religious and intellectual leaders of Manchuria, without regard to their nationality or faith, for they all admired him as a person and respected his vast knowledge in various areas of academic learning. At one time, he debated the "Merchant of Venice" and the image of Shylock with three university professors and to this day scores of men and women remember his brilliance and eloquence on that occasion.

Dr. Abraham Kaufman, the second important Jewish leader in the community, was considered by all as the authentic spokesman for and leader of local Jewish community affairs. He was responsible for organizing, indeed creating, the social and political structure of the community in Harbin and in all of China. Dr. Kaufman was born in Perm, Russia and studied medicine in Switzerland. He was one of the pioneer Zionists and served as a delegate to the Zionist Congress in Basle, Switzerland in 1899 and all his life long has been an ardent supporter of the concept of a Jewish State. He also was drafted by the Russians to serve as a doctor in World War I. He came eventually to Harbin and headed the National Jewish Council and the Far Eastern Jewish Conference. He was responsible for coordinating the social activities of the Jewish communities in China and it is no wonder that he was ranked as the top leader for Jewish affairs in the country.

In spite of his intensive community efforts, Dr. Kaufman continued his medical work and was the medical director of the Jewish Hospital of Harbin, which had over fifty beds.

The community was governed by a democratically-elected Council of forty members. In 1920, the members all represented various Zionist groups and other units which were not Zionist-oriented. The greatest representation came from the General Zionist Party, which had thirteen members on the Council. The Bund, a non-Zionist unit, had twelve members sitting on the Council. In addition, the Poale Zion, the Zeire Zion, the Mizrachi and the Agudat Israel had three members each on the Council. The Progressives had two members and the Volkspartei had one.

The Council operated under two definite and specific bases. The first was that Hebrew and Russian were to be the official languages and, second, the program and outlook of the Council were to be pro-Zionist. There were some complications involved almost immediately. It was found necessary to compromise on the language issue and to record the minutes of the meetings in Yiddish. In addition, the official letterheads were printed in three languages: Hebrew, Yiddish and English or Russian. On the matter of Zionist orientation, here the approach worked well, for the youth of Harbin accepted Zionism. The Revisionist Zionist approach was most attractive with the young people and soon Revisionism became a powerful movement and the Revisionist unit was the most active youth group in the entire Far East. The Revisionists had a militant attitude and today in Israel the Herut Party is an outgrowth of the original Revisionist party, whose philosophical leader was the brilliant Vladimir Jabotinsky.

There were two weekly magazines published by the Jewish community of Harbin. One was *Jewish Life,* issued by the General Zionists, and the second was *Hadegel* (the Flag), sponsored by the Revisionists. These periodicals reflected only one aspect of a lively cultural life. The Jews organized a music school, called *Omanut* (art), where lessons in voice and instruments were given by good teachers and competent musicians.

There also was an influential organization, called IMALDIG (the initials for *Idische, Musikalische, Literarische und Dramatische Gesellschaft*), which helped to promote culture in the community.

The Harbin Jews, however, did not focus exclusively on their own cultural development and economic expansion. A strong feeling of social consciousness existed and philanthropic and charitable institutions were warp and woof of the community fabric. Of particular value were the old age home and the shelter house, the kosher kitchen, open to Jews and non-Jews alike (where hundreds of meals were served at a very nominal cost), and the fifty-bed Jewish hospital, staffed by excellent physicians and nurses. In 1916 and through 1918, there was an attempt to establish a vocational school, but this was difficult because most of the Jewish community was engaged in trade and commerce and the Jews depended upon the Chinese for vocational skills and experience.

The educational picture was also quite bright. One had a rather wide choice for the schooling of children. For kindergarten and elementary school education there were the Talmud Torah, Russian schools or private English institutions. Most of the Jewish youths attended the high schools where subjects were taught in the Russian language. One could attend, for higher education, the English-language Y.M.C.A. College or the Russian-language Polytechnic Institute.

During their school years, the Jewish youngsters mixed freely with the Russian and Chinese students. In spite of some anti-Jewish attitudes held by the Russian youths, many individual Russians and Jews became fast friends. Sports activities and social programs were major factors in hastening and strengthening these ties.

In addition, there were two Jewish youth organizations which, in the main, provided for the youth programs. One was B'rith Trumpeldor and the second was Maccabi.

B'rith Trumpeldor was a para-military type of organization and educated its members to fight on behalf of the Jewish people, at a time when military training was generally frowned upon by Zionist leaders. This group operated under strict discipline and eventually some of its members participated in the War of Liberation which led to the creation and establishment of the modern State of Israel.

The Maccabi organization was interested primarily in sports and in the social life of its members. Although it was natural enough that there be some competition between the two groups and intense rivalries from time to time, both youth units banded together and forgot their differences in the face of any outside danger.

The harmony and unity existing between B'rith Trumpeldor and Maccabi was particularly useful in 1919, when it appeared that anti-Jewish White Russian groups would organize a series of attacks on the Jewish community. The Jewish youths, constituting a voluntary self-defense unit, managed to obtain arms and ammunition and attacked and destroyed a building in the White Russian sector of the city, which had served as the headquarters for the troublemakers. Curiously enough, the White Russians held the Jews responsible for the Communist regime in Russia. They simply did not take into account the fact that the Jews themselves were refugees from a Russia equally hostile to them. There were tensions between the two groups—sometimes erupting into violence—but on the whole, life in the 1920's was fairly peaceful. The relationship between Jews and Chinese, on the other hand, was excellent.

Harbin as a Refugee Center

Because of its strategic location and its ever-developing and expanding Russian and Jewish settlements, Harbin was a natural haven for all refugees arriving in the area from the interior of Soviet Russia. Russian cultural and social influence was obvious—and quite natural considering that so many of the refugees were from the mother country—but there was greater individual freedom in Harbin than in Russia. The Jews, in particular, enjoyed the fruits of tolerance and liberty.

A brief survey of some Jewish history is, at this point, of some significance and will prove to be helpful in understanding the Jewish situation in Harbin.

The main contribution of the Jews to Russia's pioneering effort in Manchuria—prior to the Russian Revolution in 1917—was by helping to construct the Chinese Eastern Railway. Within Czarist Russia, the Jews were stifled and discriminated against. The bias against them existed not only politically, but economically as well. One result of this anti-Semitism was the inability of the Jew to take part in Russian politics and economy. Those Jews who did manage to succeed in either or both spheres were the exceptions rather than the rule. In the main, the Jews in Czarist Russia learned to expect that they had practically no chance for advancement.

But the patterns of behavior were radically different in Manchuria. The Russian brand of anti-Semitism was not for export, at least not officially. When Czarist Russia planned the railway and the economic expansion of Manchuria, the Jews were encouraged to play a major role in this effort and—at least on this level, and at this time—the bias the Government may have had against the Jews was not apparent. It is clear, then, that the Jews who settled in Manchuria before the revolution did so out of the knowledge that in that faraway land they would have a degree of freedom hitherto unknown to them.

Then there came the Russian Revolution. Much has been written about the history of this momentous event, for it has changed our entire world and the changes are taking place to this day. What has been reported only by Jewish historians, however, is the heavy toll taken of Jewish life in this revolution. The civil war in Russia and the terrible pogroms in the Ukraine alone took more than 60,000 Jewish lives. Those who survived the holocaust began to look about for new homes in new lands, where they could bind up their wounds and begin life anew.

Many of them dreamed of coming to the United States, which had absorbed so many of their relatives and friends before the War. The United States was still the *"goldene medina,"* the golden land, for the immigration policies were still liberal and the refugees had every reason to wish to come to America. Nevertheless, there were obstacles and problems. Within Russia itself there were transportation shortages, while Western European ports, due to the War, were just about closed to commercial traffic.

These obstacles were too much for many refugees who then undertook the long and arduous trek across Russia by way of the Trans-Siberian Railroad. All along the road, and especially at Irkutsk, Harbin and the port of Vladivostok, these travelers were aided by Jews who, only a little while before, were homeless refugees themselves.

This well-intended aid was good so far as it went, but it was not really enough. There were literally thousands upon thousands of refugees, many of them women and children (whose male relatives had escaped to the United States). They had nowhere to turn, for they did not even know where their relatives were located in the countries abroad which had welcomed them. An immediate result was that many of the wanderers were stuck in the port cities of Vladivostok and in Yokohama, Japan. The traffic of refugees piled up. The women and children, without husbands and fathers, were most helpless. But the men, too, could do little for themselves. They all hoped to board a vessel when they reached Vladivostok or Yokohama, but without money, friends or contacts, they merely sat around. The situation became critical.

The HIAS (Hebrew Immigrant Aid Society) decided that it had to step into this perilous situation. Thus, HIAS sent to Japan its able chairman on Foreign Relations, Samuel Mason, who came to Japan early in 1918. Mason quickly realized that it was necessary for him to visit Manchuria and Siberian Russia if he was to solve certain emigration problems on the spot.

It was under these complex conditions that HIAS' Far Eastern operations came into motion. Mason's reports of 1918 provide an excellent and vivid account of the chaotic conditions existing at that time. Many of the refugees were robbed by swindlers, exploited by thieves and opium traffickers in Harbin. Living conditions were terribly bad and the refugees lived in filthy, crowded quarters and in cellars in Vladivostok. Because of the traffic jam-up, they were forced to live under these unpleasant, unhygienic conditions for as long as ten months. Then, if they were lucky, they were able to move on.

Another valuable insight into the conditions under which the Jews had to survive is offered in a report to Louis Marshall, made on June 10, 1918. Mr. Marshall is no longer remembered by many people today, although he was one of the most important Jewish leaders of his time. He was a distinguished constitutional lawyer and the chairman of the American Jewish Committee. He also served with distinction as a member of the Jewish delegation to the Versailles Peace Conference of 1919. A few years ago, a two-volume edition of Mr. Marshall's letters was published by the Jewish Publication Society and the reader is impressed by the enormous influence wielded by Mr. Marshall in the days when he was the outstanding leader of the Jewish community in America.

The report to Mr. Marshall emphasized the insecure status of the Jews in Russia, for they were being blamed for the success of the Communists in Russia. The accusation was made that Jewish aid and support helped Communism make headway in Russia. The fact is that these charges were totally untrue. This can be easily proved by the result of the all-Jewish Congress held in Russia between January 7 and 9 in 1918. Some sixty-five per cent of the voters selected Zionist delegates, twelve per cent chose religious-orthodox representatives and twenty-three per cent made their choice of the remaining groups and parties. Obviously, there was no overwhelming support for the Communists among the Jews. This situation held for the Far Eastern district of Russia as well, and this section included the Manchurian colonies and Harbin. The General Zionists received 2,400 votes, the Bund 300, the People's Party 181 and the Poale Zion 180. The General Zionists represented the middle class and business circles and the others tended to lean toward labor. All, however, were intensely interested in strengthening the Jewish community in the area.

The Bolsheviks were so unhappy and dissatisfied with the results that they sought to prevent the convocation of the assembly and to prohibit the publication of the election results on the ground that even making the vote public was a counter-revolutionary act. Hatred for the Soviet regime was especially violent in Manchuria, whose de facto government was composed of the administrators of the Chinese Eastern Railway.

The HIAS and DALJEWCIB

In the face of this uncertainty, the unstable political conditions and the crowded communal plight of so many of the Jews, it remains a remarkable feat that Samuel Mason was able to establish information bureaus in Irkutsk, Harbin and Vladivostok. While the others were dissolved in time, the Harbin office continued to function until 1939, when it had to transfer to Shanghai. The other relief agencies operated in this area for a brief period, only until 1922 or 1923. The agencies were the Joint Distribution Committee (the JDC), the American Relief Administration (AMA) and the DEKOPO, an agency which dedicated itself to the care of Jewish children who were orphaned as a result of the pogroms in Russia.

The HIAS, which had world-wide fame, was known in the area as DALJEWCIB, the letters standing for the Far Eastern Jewish Central Information Bureau.

In order to understand and appreciate the enormous labors of this bureau, one has to study and remember the statistics which are available concerning the work of the DALJEWCIB. From 1918 to 1934, a period of sixteen years, this bureau processed 68,566 applications for emigration, documentation of citizenship and searches for relatives of would-be emigrants. More than 16,000 applied for emigration alone. Papers were prepared for 15,384 of these persons. More than 10,000 were sent abroad and 417 relatives were transferred from Eastern Europe to their families in the Far East. At the same time, thousands upon thousands of food parcels were transmitted to needy relatives in Eastern Europe and Russia. In American money, $134,468 was spent in cash contributions for those who needed the money. Finally, 29,528 tracers were sent out for missing relatives, of which 16,246 resulted in successful contacts.

These figures tend to blur the human element. There are agony and heartbreak, sadness and misery hidden behind these statistics. Simultaneously, there are hope and joy, new life and opportunities for new families—but these can be appreciated only by those men and women who were aided when help was necessary to their survival, not only as human beings but as Jews as well.

The entire rescue operation is a highlight of the HIAS organization and special credit is due to its hard-working Far

Eastern manager, M. Birman. These outstanding humanitarian activities also reflect the wonderful spirit of hospitality of the Far Eastern Russian Jews who lived in Harbin. They opened their homes and their hearts to the unfortunate refugees, who had to wait months and years before they could be placed in homes elsewhere in the world. Thus, there was a constant coming and going, steady movement, within Harbin itself. Yet fruitful as these activities were, these were only minor compared with the work that was to be done a few years later as a result of the Japanese occupation of Manchuria in 1932 and the growth of Nazism in Germany and Eastern Europe in the 1930's.

Japanese Occupation of Manchuria

The period from the end of World War I until 1932 has been called the "Golden Era of the Jews in China." This high-flown description is well justified by the events of the following years. The first years of the Japanese occupation were filled with violence and political instability, accompanied by an economic squeeze by the Japanese on all foreign interests. The invaders forced many export-import firms, and their representatives, to look for greater economic freedom and opportunity elsewhere and they found it, more often than not, in the international cities of Shanghai and Tientsin. A great many of the businessmen forced to look for new horizons were the Jews.

It has been correctly stated that the first battles of World War II were fought in remote Manchuria. The conflicting countries were Soviet Russia and Japan. Prior to 1931, both nations had established large industries in the area which was officially recognized as part of China, and so it was natural that sooner or later these massive powers would face each other as foes in the Far East.

Japan had used the Kwantung Army to penetrate Manchuria.

Originally, this military force was simply a unit of men guarding the South Manchurian Railway. In time, however, the Kwantung Army became one of the most powerful instrumentalities used by the Japanese expansionists. The top officers of the Army considered themselves to be more than mere military leaders; they also were political leaders. As members of the Supreme Command of the Japanese Army, they were responsible directly to the Emperor and no one else. The Mukden incident—an explosion near the Mukden railway—had been engineered by the Army and in the fighting that followed, Manchukuo was formed. Technically an independent state, Manchukuo was in truth a puppet state manipulated by its Japanese masters.

The Mukden incident aroused the conscience of the League of Nations which was, in a sense, the forerunner of the United Nations, and the League undertook to debate the Mukden incident at Geneva. On the basis of the League's castigation of Japan's actions, Japan withdrew from the League, thus beginning the end of the League's influence on the world scene.

Quite apart from Japan's official violation of human rights, there were bandit groups in Harbin and Manchuria that wreaked havoc in those territories and created an atmosphere of terror. It became impossible for ordinary human beings to walk the streets with impunity and one required a bodyguard or a gun for safety's sake. In 1932 and 1933 this banditry reached its peak, with kidnappings and killings a daily occurrence. Naturally, the chief targets of the kidnappers were the wealthy men, some of whom were Jewish. The ransom demands were staggering, as illustrated in the internationally-famous Kaspe affair.

Amleto Vespa was an adventurous Italian correspondent who was in the employ of the Manchurian police and later was an agent for the Japanese. In his volume, *Secret Agent of Japan*, Vespa offers many pages of "inside information" on the Kaspe case and other exciting cases.

Simon Kaspe was a talented pianist, the son of rich parents living in Harbin. Joseph Kaspe, Simon's father, had become a French citizen because he wanted to protect his vast holdings. Simon Kaspe was kidnapped and murdered. Because Joseph Kaspe was now French, the French Vice Consul undertook to investigate the circumstances connected with the killing of Simon Kaspe. According to Vespa's account, the Japanese, yielding to public and world-wide pressure, managed to apprehend the criminals and place them on trial before a Chinese court, which condemned the killers for their crimes.

It seemed that the case was at an end. But it was not, for after a while, the Japanese arrested the Chinese judges who had condemned the bandits to prison and released the convicts. The Japanese praised the killers as patriots who had killed Simon Kaspe after kidnapping him in an attempt to raise funds for anti-Communist organizations.

The files of the Japanese Foreign Office contain a number of protests on the case, made by N. E. B. Ezra, editor of *Israel's Messenger*, a Shanghai monthly established in 1904. Mr. Ezra had written to M. Shigemitsu, the Japanese Vice Minister—and sometimes Acting Minister—for Foreign Affairs. Mr. Ezra referred to the Kaspe case and the agitation of the White Russians who imported European anti-Semitism. He pointed out that the White Russian periodical, the *Nashput*, was violently anti-Jewish and identified Jews with Communists and blamed them for the murder of the Czar.

Mr. Ezra followed up his letters with a personal visit to the Foreign Office in Tokyo, where he was received by Shigemitsu on August 24, 1934. He was assured by the Japanese that the Japanese government would take "steps to suppress lawless agitation in Harbin." The fearless editor, in a later letter to Dr. Oyabe, a personal friend in the Foreign Office, complained that Shigemitsu had done nothing to improve the situation in spite of his assurances. The letter to Dr. Oyabe was written on November 2, 1934, which means that some three months had elapsed with no action taken.

The situation in Harbin was particularly tense and unpleasant mainly because the Chief of Police, Mr. Eguchi, was biased against the Jews and had released a slanderous report on the Jews of Harbin. In general, the Tokyo authorities were not at all pleased with this unfavorable publicity, particularly since they were interested in accepting 50,000 German Jews for resettlement in Manchuria. This ambitious plan had been announced by Yotaro Sugimura, a former director of the political section of the League of Nations and a spokesman for the Japanese Government.

In Jewish circles, this Japanese plan for accepting 50,000 Jews was interpreted as being motivated for two prime reasons: 1) to aid the development of Manchuria for the benefit of Japan and 2) to help build up a large Jewish community to compete with the Russian-Jewish state of Biro-Bidjan, which lay across the Russian border in Siberia.

The Japanese Foreign Office was disturbed over the unfriendly reports that had spread over the world in relation to the treatment of the Jews. As a result, the office sent a letter to the Harbin consulate informing them that they had been receiving inquiries from their New York and Chinese consulates on the Harbin situation.

The diplomatic exchanges revealed that there was indeed in Harbin a Russian Fascist association led by a man named Rodzaevsky and Eguchi, the police chief who had labelled as patriots the Kaspe murderers. In another report—from Morito Morishima the Harbin Consul General—to Jiro Minami, the Japanese Ambassador in Manchuria, it was made clear that a meeting was held by officials of Harbin with leaders of the Jewish community. The meeting was called in order to discover ways and means to ease the tensions in the city which were caused by anti-Semitism.

One result of the meeting was a series of newspaper articles on the subject. In one of the articles, this statement was made: "Japan and Manchuria have no reason to oppress the Jewish people, who will have the protection of the state so long as they behave according to the regulations of Manchuria."

But Jewish activities to calm the ruffled waters did not halt with this meeting. The Shanghai Jewish Communal Association held a mass meeting on December 18, 1934 and protested to the Foreign Office in Tokyo on the matter of the treatment of the Jewish people. Those who signed the declaration of protest, in addition to Mr. Ezra, were Rabbi M. Ashkenazi, B. Topaz and H. Epstein. It is evident, on the basis of the complaint lodged by Mr. Ezra, that the major Harbin synagogue and the home of Rabbi Levin had been raided on Yom Kippur, the Day of Atonement and the holiest day of the Jewish calendar year (on October 7, 1935) by Japanese officials looking for "arms and banned literature."

In an open letter to the editor of the *Shanghai Times*, on October 30, 1935, Mr. Ezra called for a public apology for this flagrant disrespect for the Jewish people and their holy day. In addition, the Joint Committee of the British Jewish Board of Deputies and the Anglo-Jewish Association filed an official protest on April 29, 1936, with the Japanese Ambassador in Great Britain for anti-Jewish demonstrations by the White Russians in Harbin and for the wholesale arrest of Jewish businessmen who were "charged with fictitious offenses in order to force them to offer bribes." A similar protest was lodged by the American Jewish Committee with the Japanese Ambassador in Washington and the president of the Committee publicly expressed the hope that Japan would take appropriate action to improve the situation.

A major source of the anti-Semitic propaganda against which these organizations were complaining was the Russian Bureau of Emigrants' Affairs, the official agency for Russian emigrants which had been organized by the Japanese in 1934. These White Russians were anti-Jewish and many of them had been officers in the Czar's army. They still entertained the hope that the Japanese invasion of Manchuria would lead to the invasion of Siberia and the eventual overthrow of the Soviet government. The nominal head of the Bureau was General Kislitsin, although its most active leader was Rodzaevsky, its deputy chief, and the head of the Russian Fascist Association, probably the most aggressive anti-Semitic unit in Manchuria.

The foregoing history of protest, mass meetings and diplomatic activity indicates how deeply affected the Jews of Manchuria were by the new and dangerous political and economic trends and developments. It had started, at the outset, with the Jews being victimized by bandits and White Russian fascists who robbed, kidnapped and killed in order to raise funds for their propaganda activities. It already has been stressed that it was dangerous for the Jews to walk the streets of the cities in the territory. It also has been pointed out that the economic situation of the Jews was worsening. And it has been emphasized that Harbin itself, as the center of the Chinese Eastern Railway administration and as the center for the soy bean trade, had attracted thousands of White Russians. Obviously, these trends were to lead to peril for the Jews.

There were, in addition to the Jews, other foreigners and they, too, were now in an insecure position. Tientsin, the hub of the Chinese and Mongolian fur export trade, also had many foreigners. Dairen, a free port, had its share of foreigners—and all of them had little or no contact with the millions of Chinese living in the interior of the country.

The foreigners themselves can be divided into two categories. The first group consisted of those who were citizens of treaty powers, such as the United States, England and France. These lands had their own concessions, extra-territorial rights, armies, police and complete jurisdiction over their own nationals. The second group of foreigners were citizens of non-treaty powers, East Europeans or stateless individuals.

On this basis, it is easy to understand why foreigners with treaty power status were important in the development of the country. They operated under the protection of their own governments and had the time to become acquainted (if they were early settlers) with the Chinese traders and get along with them. A foreigner, in general, was limited in his opportunities and tried to get along in the export-import business. It was impossible for a foreigner to compete with the Chinese in production because Chinese labor was so amazingly cheap.

The Sale of the Chinese Eastern Railway

Quite clearly, foreigners depended upon other foreigners as customers, and when there was a radical change in the economy, Jewish tradesmen suffered heavily. A case in point is the history of the Chinese Eastern Railway, which was sold by the Soviets to the Japanese. This road, it will be recalled, had been the key instrumentality of Russia's penetration into the Far East and Manchuria. It employed thousands of Russian workmen who, in turn, were excellent customers for local businessmen, including, of course, the Jews. Technically, the railway was sold to the Manchurian authorities; in reality, Japan itself bought the road, through its puppets in Manchukuo, for 170,000,000 yen.

Almost immediately, the Japanese changed the gauge of the road to that of the South Manchurian railroad, for this move enabled the Japanese to travel more swiftly from Japanese-held Manchuria into former Russian-held territory.

One of the initial results of the sale of the railway to Japan was the loss of jobs for 20,000 railway employees, who returned to Russia in 1935. Their evacuation led, at first, to a rise in the sale of consumer goods, for these people took back with them a wide selection of goods to Russia. In the long run, however, the departure of these 20,000 workers harmed the local Jewish tradesmen. Since there were very few Jews employed by the railway, it may be assumed that only a handful of those who went back to Russia were Jewish.

As for the Jewish populace of Harbin itself, most of the Jews had come to the city after they crossed—illegally—from Siberia into Manchuria via the Amur River. This emigration had begun in 1931, when Soviet Russia tightened its own borders and introduced new laws against citizens leaving Russia.

With the decline of the economy in Harbin, the Jews were forced to turn elsewhere in order to earn a living. The two cities which were large and had Jewish communities operating under the free enterprise system were Tientsin and Shanghai. This is the reason why 2,000 Harbin Jews moved to Tientsin and another 4,000 to 5,000 went to Shanghai. This heavy emigration reduced the Jewish population of Harbin from 13,000 in 1929 to 8,000 in 1935, to 5,000 in 1939.

There are additional statistics available which offer an interesting insight into the expanding Japanese penetration of the area and the resulting displacement of foreign interests. On the eve of the Japanese occupation of Manchuria in 1931 and 1932, fifty-eight per cent of Harbin's private industries were owned by Chinese capital; thirty-three per cent by non-Soviet Russians and Russians Jews, eight per cent by the Japanese and one per cent by American and Western European interests. Russian Jews controlled large segments of the grain and lumber trades and other commercial industries.

Yet in 1934, only two years after the Japanese moved in, the Japanese held all the ship-building enterprises in the city, as well as many of the soya bean and the flour mills. They reorganized the grain exchange, and forced Kabalkin to resign his post. Although this was mentioned earlier, it is worth stressing at this juncture once again. By 1939, therefore, the Japanese owned twelve per cent of all the most important industries, handling some thirty per cent of the entire trade in Harbin.

Those who were lucky enough to get out of Harbin had deep feelings about their Judaism. Of course, they often succeeded in moving their physical assets to the large cities of Tientsin and Shanghai. But more than that: they created new Jewish communities so that they could live as Jews in their new homes. A typical example is that of the Tientsin Hebrew Association. Until 1930, this association was run by a committee headed by a fur-dealer from Irkutsk named Leo Gershevich. Mr. Gershevich was self-educated and keenly aware of the need for Jewish culture in a land which, until that time, had been without Jews. He soon collected enough books to boast of one of the finest private libraries in the city. Within a brief span of time, Tientsin had an impressive synagogue, a school and a club and the members of these units enjoyed friendly relations with the Chinese and other foreign residents of the city.

Curiously, the Japanese were unhappy over the Jewish exodus from Harbin. As early as December, 1935, Shoshiro Sato, the Japanese Consul General in Harbin, submitted a consular police report to Jiro Minami, the Japanese Ambassador in Manchuria, in which he emphasized the need for a change on the part of the local authorities in relation to their anti-Jewish attitude. He asserted that an altered attitude would contribute towards the "utilization of the Jews" who would otherwise leave Manchuria "to seek better places for peaceful living." By "utilization," Sato meant "foreign capital," which was of prime interest to the Japanese and a key factor in their appraisal of its Jews. At this time, Japan had embarked on its New Order in East Asia and it desperately required all the human and economic resources it could pool in order to attain its objectives in Manchuria and China.

The need for new resources became particularly critical in 1937, with the outbreak of the Sino-Japanese conflict. This war prompted the Western Powers to convene the Brussels Conference in November, 1937 in an attempt to seek means of conciliation between the enemy factions. The results were inconclusive—disastrous from the Western point of view—and revealed the lack of unity among the Western nations. In addition, the failure of the conference discredited the concept of taking collective action against Japan. What was even worse was that this failure strengthened the Japanese belief in the correctness of their policy and encouraged the Army leaders to continue their drive into Manchuria and China.

Although Japan felt sufficiently independent to reject an invitation to attend the conference, it did not consider itself strong enough to get along without foreign capital—and the Japanese leaders still took into account world public opinion. Thus, the Nipponese—like the Russian Czarist regime before them—tried to utilize the Jews in expanding the economy of Manchuria and did what they could to exploit Jewish "know-how" for their own benefit.

The Japanese were realistic enough to understand that in order to win over the Jews to their side they would have to offer something new, something more substantial than promises alone. They knew that what the Jews wanted was political status.

The Russian Jews of Manchuria and China felt acutely the lack of political status. Although they spoke the Russian language and lived like Russians in habit and custom, they did not feel truly protected by the Russians both before and after the 1917 revolution. The great majority of the Jews were middle-class in outlook and they heartily disliked and distrusted the Communist regime. They always considered themselves to be a Jewish national minority, inspired by the concept of Jewish peoplehood, and were Zionist-oriented. That is to say, they looked forward to the establishment of a Jewish homeland in Palestine.

In 1938, this unit of Jews issued a Statement of Aims (to be found in the archives of the American Jewish Committee) and

in it, they called themselves "fragments of an invisible nation."
There was no talk, of course, about an "agreement" between
Japan and the Jews, for the very formulation of the term "agree-
ment" would imply formal arrangements between equals and the
Japanese had not yet come to that point.

Yet the Japanese were aware that Jews could still emigrate
to other parts of China or overseas and they did not want to lose
these Jews. They therefore wanted to work out some kind and
degree of cooperation on a voluntary basis. In gaining the cooperation of the Jews of Harbin, the Japanese must also have
hoped to reach the former Harbin residents now living in Tientsin, Shanghai and other sections of China. In this fashion, they
hoped to "coordinate" the entire Jewish community, and to win
a better impression abroad.

It is under these conditions that a three-day conference was
called—and the reader can surmise as to who took the initiative,
the Jews or the Japanese, as the Japanese had much to gain
from any agreement that could be worked out. On the other
hand, the Japanese wished the world to believe that the Jews
sought the conference. Twenty-one delegates from Tientsin,
Mukden, Hailar and Kobe, Japan, came to the conference. A
Japanese Foreign Office report states that the Jews approached
the authorities for permission to initiate the conference so as to
come to a better understanding of Japan's political objectives
and to reaffirm a common stand against Communism. On the
other hand, contemporary reports insist that the Japanese organized the conference and, indeed, just about directed the Jewish
communities to send delegates to it. Much of the information
on this historical issue is buried in the personal files and in the
memories of the Jewish participants, and only some of the information has been forthcoming.

There is another expert opinion available on this matter. It
was reported in an article in *Gesher*, a quarterly published by
the World Jewish Congress in Israel, by S. Rabinovitch, in 1957.

The essay was entitled "The Jewish Settlement in China, Its Development and Destruction." According to Mr. Rabinovitch, the era from 1932–1945 was a period of *Shtadlanut*. A *Shtadlan* is an elected or self-appointed Jewish emissary pleading the cause of his people before the authorities. This period witnessed a massive communal effort to aid the local Jews out of necessity, and not out of admiration or love for the Japanese. There never was full trust on either side, as Jews and Japanese met and negotiated.

The agenda for all the meetings at the conference were prepared by the Japanese, with a Colonel Senko Yasue as the chief liaison officer representing the occupation authorities. Many top officials attended the conference as well as 700 members of the Harbin Jewish community. Here are some of the officials who participated: Brigadier General Higuchi, Chief, Special Service (Intelligence), Manchuria; Vice Governor Seintaro Yuuki of Hong Kong Province; Colonel Senko Yasue, Army Central Headquarters; Major Kawamura, Provost Marshal, Chief, Special Service Section; Major Onucci, Special Service, Japan; Vice Consul Taniguchi of the Japanese Consulate; Tomoji Usui, Chief, Special Section, Police Division, Hong Kong; Chief Saito, Foreign Affairs Section, Police Station; S. Skidelsky, Honorary Portuguese Consul; General Vrashevsky, Representative of White Russian General Semiyonov and General Haksheef, Chief, Japanese Russian Administration Bureau.

A proclamation was read and a resolution proposed extolling the new spirit of cooperation between the Jewish people and the peoples of Manchuria and Japan. It is an interesting commentary on the situation that General Higuchi urged the representatives at the conference to give the proclamation active support and not to regard it as "a dead statement." He must have been aware that before the Jews could truly abide by the spirit of the resolution suspicion had to be overcome—and that complete cooperation could not exist unless and until suspicion was actually overcome. The General extolled the Jewish people and offered praiseworthy statements concerning Jewish history. He spoke of the Jewish contribution to science and economics. The reason for Jewish troubles in the world, he said, were due to the fact that the Jews did not have a national home of their own and because the Jews refused to become assimilated. He declared that all Jewish problems could readily be solved with the establishment of a Jewish homeland and with opportunities given to Jews to develop their capabilities in the fields of science and economy in the lands of their residence. He also stated that Japan was not interested in fighting against the Chinese but against Communism in China—and he hoped that the Jews would aid in this battle.

According to the report, all the delegates were delighted over the General's remarks and hope was expressed that the basic problems of the Jews in the Far East would be solved.

On the basis of the report, there were three fundamental problems facing the Jews:

1. The establishment of a pattern of self-government.

2. The creation of a unified policy concerning all religious, cultural, national and social questions.

3. The acceptance of a policy in support of a Jewish national homeland in Palestine.

The first session of the conference was in the nature of a public meeting, carefully-staged and well-attended. It was not intended to deal deeply or seriously with significant issues. The second session, however, was devoted to internal and organizational Jewish problems. By this time, attendance had melted to 120, but the delegates took their responsibilities most seriously and a study of the activities of the delegates reveals that the conference was more than a mere tool for the Japanese. There were serious debates on the scope of the responsibilities of the conference. Some delegates felt that only national and secular issues should be considered. Others believed that religious issues had to be included in any discussion for one could not separate the Jew into a national entity apart from his religion. As an

outgrowth of this session—and based on clear and useful thinking—a decision was reached that all the Jewish communities
would be combined into a single overall autonomous association.
In order to make sure that the new association would understand
its duties and the purposes for which it was being created, the
delegates reached agreement on the areas of interest which the
association would cover. It was wide and broad:

1. All religious problems, including issues that arose within
the synagogue, or within the personal religious lives of the Jews,
or with the spiritual leaders attempting to guide the Jewish
community along religious lines.

2. All educational and cultural activities, with special emphasis on schools, libraries, magazines and other publications.

3. Social and economic activities, including the establishment of a cooperative union and a fund-raising organization.

4. To support orphanages and shelters and to care for
refugees who arrived from Central Europe.

5. To encourage and promote physical education of the
young people as a means of assuring their health and alertness.

6. To register all Jews as well as Jewish organizations and
to take a census of the Jewish population and to record all births,
deaths and marriages.

The association was to be authorized to collect funds for its
maintenance and to carry out its program. The example of Germany was used here, for it was shown that in Germany taxes
were collected through state officials and then turned over to
Jewish leaders for the maintenance of Jewish communities. The
governing body of the association was also to be authorized to
deal with government officials in Japan and Manchuria. In
addition, the association would give vigorous support to the
Zionist program to establish a Jewish homeland in Palestine.

There also was discussion on the question of observance of
ritual laws and on the Sabbath. This debate was introduced by
Rabbi Kiseleff and it is intriguing to discover that the items that

came up, the depth of the discussions and the heat of the debate are reminiscent of some of the controversy on religion that later arose in the State of Israel on precisely the same matters. In any event, the delegates agreed unanimously that maximum religious observance was a necessity.

It was decided that Harbin would be the permanent headquarters for a national council for all the Jewish community associations in the Far East. Each community with a minimum of twenty-five Jewish families was entitled to one delegate.

The third day of the conference was devoted to the cultural and educational problems facing the association. All communities were urged to stress the teaching of the Hebrew language and of Jewish history and culture. It was also pointed out that the children should be taught Russian and Japanese as well, for considering the environment in which the Jews lived, these "exotic" languages were necessary adjuncts to Jewish life in the Far East.

It is obvious by this time that the report on the activities of the conference was lengthy and thorough. It was concluded with the observations made by Captain Inuzuka of the Third Section, Navy, and a Japanese "expert" on the "Jewish question." The captain made these four particular points:

1. It was recognized that the purpose of the conference had been attained.

2. It was regrettable that representatives from Shanghai and Hong Kong would not attend the conference.

3. In view of the peculiar nature of the Jews (religious exclusivity, Jewish relations with other nationalities, Jewish "self-complacency,") one could not be certain that the results of the conference—while they appeared to be good ones—would last.

4. It was apparent that serious thought had to be given as to the treatment of the Jews of Shanghai and Hong Kong, because these Jews did not support the Jap-invasion of China. It was the hope of the Japanese that the results of the con-

ference, its tone and its "success," would help persuade the Jews to favor Japan and to support its New Order in China.

It is now known that Sir Victor Sassoon, one of the most influential Jewish leaders in the Far East, was closely watched by the Japanese. The Sassoon family wielded great power in the East, in India as well as in Shanghai and other corners of the Orient. When Sir Victor stopped over in Tokyo for one day (July 13, 1939), Japanese agents shadowed him. He talked with a passport examiner, and this conversation was also noted. His views on British-Japanese disagreements were duly reported to the Japanese ministries of Interior and Commerce. Actually, Sir Victor's views were forthright and by no means surprising. He urged that the problems involved be handled through diplomatic channels and rejected the idea of using military force to reach decisions. He stated that if his companies in Asia could not be managed properly because of interference, he would move his business out of the area.

In a report (dated February 18, 1939) the Japanese Consul General in New York expressed his opinion that Sir Victor Sassoon already had cleared his properties out of China and that he no longer was the top Jewish financier in the region, having yielded that position to the Hardoons.

The Japanese Foreign Office was quite busy in keeping tabs on the Jews in the locality and it has been discovered that Mr. M. Speelman, the chairman of the Finance Committee for Jewish Refugees, was also watched rather closely. He was labelled as "a magnate among the French comparable to Sassoon among the English."

Between Conferences

Following the first conference, there was a second, and then a third. The period between the first and third conference evoked some controversy and mixed reactions among various groups within Manchuria on the value and significance of these meetings.

A typical reaction was that of the White Russians. They appeared to be jealous over the new status gained by the Jews, according to a Foreign Office report from Tsitsihar. The Jews, it seemed clear to the White Russians, were now considered independent of the White Russians. Some of the Russian leaders felt that they should overcome their own animus toward the Jews and support the Japanese policies. Others went so far as to concede that if the Manchurian government allowed the Jews to live in peace and security, these same Jews would invest heavy sums of money in Manchurian industry—to the benefit of the White Russians themselves. There was a third view: that the Japanese sincerely wished to help the Jews establish a homeland, for the lack of a country made the Jews "evil." Finally, there was a missionary viewpoint: that the new Jewish status was an expression of the Manchurian national spirit. Yet those who held this opinion also felt that the Jews had to be watched constantly because they were "an international race."

It cannot be said, in retrospect, that the Far Eastern conference made it easier for large numbers of refugees to settle in Manchuria. At best, only a few hundred refugees were permitted entry. The official policy of non-admittance was clearly stated in a letter from Zai Yung Sheng, the Director-General of the Manchurian Foreign Office, to Yan Chen Zhe, the Manchurian Ambassador to Japan. The epistle, dated January 19, 1940, deals with Manchukuo's attitude on the influx of Jews into Shanghai. It refers to Enclosures A and B as evidence of Manchukuo's policy toward the refugees. Enclosure A is a copy of a telegram, dated October 29, 1938, from the Prime Minister to the Minister to Italy, and it expresses "the fear that any admission of Jewish refugees purged by our allied countries may have an undesirable effect upon our diplomatic relations with the allied countries and threaten our diplomatic interests. Therefore, we will, in a roundabout way, refuse admission except for applicants with special skills, such as engineers and those who have never been engaged in a political movement or organization and so are recognized to be harmless and permitted to reside in our country."

This was not all. The text continues: "In putting this policy into force it is desirable—with a view to a possible effect upon our policy for the Jewish people in Manchuria—that the applicants should, if necessary, be dissuaded from their intentions for settlement in Manchuria by the reason of the difficulty of foreigners' life here. This is not meant to prevent issuance of transit visas for those who bear visas for other countries."

This policy of refusal in a "roundabout way" was restated in another letter—written on May 1, 1939—by the Director General of the Foreign Affairs Bureau to the heads of the subordinate divisions. In fact, the granting of any visas, for entry or transit, had now become the concern of the Foreign Affairs Bureau itself. Up to this time, the decisions were made by the local visa offices. This new step indicated that there was to be a further tightening of visa procedures.

As a result of these regulation changes, there was little movement into or out of Manchuria until December 23, 1939, when Manchurian authorities somewhat relaxed their policies. The Manchurian officials moved as they did because the Japanese themselves led the way. The Japanese had made it easier, in many ways, for those persons whom they had allowed into their army-occupied area of the international settlement of Shanghai. Thus, the Manchurian Ambassador to Japan was authorized to issue transit visas through Manchuria to those applicants who had received entrance permits issued by the Municipal Council of the International or French Settlement and those who had Japanese transit visas for the Canton province.

The Japanese were quite explicit in their instructions to the Manchurian Ambassador and in their authorization to him, they

referred to "quite a number of refugees who, with their persist-
ent request for Manchurian visas, had been a cause of trouble
for the authorities in Dairen." The statement attempted to clarify
the matter in greater detail: "They are the refugees from
Shanghai who, because of the difficult living conditions there,
contacted their Jewish acquaintances in Manchuria for an employment contract; then they arrived unwelcomed in Dairen to
claim a Manchurian visa by virtue of their contract. Hereafter,
it is desired that such refugees who are suspected of going to
Dairen only for the purpose of entering Manchukuo, should not
be issued Canton visas by the Japanese authorities unless they
have authorization by the Manchurian visa office in Shanghai."

The Jews living in Manchuria did all within their power to
persuade and influence the local authorities to act more favorably toward the Jewish refugees. This is evident from a Jewish
report filed in the Japanese Foreign Office together with other
Japanese General Staff documents (dated July 7, 1938). The
report itself contains material taken from an article entitled
"Japan and the Jewish People," which was published in the
periodical *Jewish Life,* the official organ of the Far Eastern Conference. The article was written "to offset the anti-Japan propaganda of some European papers prompted by an alleged
anti-Jewish movement in Japan." The very fact that Jews had
been free to organize themselves was cited as proof that the
Japanese offered equal treatment to all foreigners, including
Jews.

The National Council had more ambitious aims. Its leaders
realized that it would be helpful if the leaders of American
Jewish organizations would become familiar with the facts of
Jewish life in Manchuria, with emphasis on the tolerance ex-
hibited by Japanese and Manchurian authorities. A number of
important Jewish businessmen from the area visited the United
States and met with Dr. Cyrus Adler, president of the American
Jewish Committee, and with Rabbi Stephen S. Wise, president

of the American Jewish Congress, in order to acquaint them with
the situation *vis à vis* the Jews in the Far East.

The Jewish leaders of the Far East hoped, in these talks, to
convince the American Jewish spokesmen to think better of
Japan. An October, 1938 report issued by the Far Eastern Council, for example, makes it a cardinal point to stress the political
equality of the Jewish residents in Manchuria and Japan. It
continues by emphasizing that Jews were participating in all
areas of industry and commerce.

The 1938 report also stressed that Jews, and all other national minorities, enjoyed complete religious and cultural freedom. An illustration given was the existence of the Jewish school
in Harbin. Here is the text of the passage on this school: "Lately,
in Manchu-Ti-Kuo, school reform was carried out and all schools
had to be run by the government or the municipality, with a
common program for all of the schools. But in answer to a petition of the National Council, the Jewish school was left in the
hands of the Jewish community, with its own former program,
namely, its national-religious program."

On the problem of anti-Semitism, the report observed: "Gov-
ernmental anti-Semitism does not exist here. There is no anti-
Semitic movement, either. In Manchu-Ti-Kuo, a group of
Russian emigrants attempted to introduce anti-Semitism and to
provoke it in the area. This group even had its own anti-Semitic
newspaper in Harbin, called *Nash Poot* (Our Way), which
spread the usual calumnies about Jews. This edition was closed
by the authorities in 1937 and does not appear any more." The
report included the full text of General Higuchi's speech to the
First Conference of 1937 and concluded with these remarks:
"Sincerely and in all justice, we may number Manchu-Ti-Kuo
and Japan among the few countries where we Jews do not suffer
from any limitations and injustices; where the Jewish national
minority is given civic equality as well as the right to cultural
development."

Up to this point, I have been quoting from historical documents and from newspaper reports and official statements by government spokesmen and leaders of the Jewish community. All of this documentation is of extreme value and significance in evaluating the trends in Jewish life and history during this critical and significant era.

But, from time to time, I must—as an observer and historian myself—digress to make a point, to take issue with some of the documentation, or to highlight errors in fact or emphasis.

This is, I believe, an appropriate moment to state that I must express my doubts as to the accuracy and the sincerity of the report quoted above or, for that matter, on any official report of that time which had to pass the sharp eyes of the Japanese censors. Still, it is not easy to determine just how much propaganda and how much wishful thinking are incorporated in this report.

Some of its findings and claims were re-stated and even intensified in an eleven-page statement of the Council to the American Jewish Committee. I do not hesitate to quote from the statement because it reflects the thinking of those Jews who believed in greater cooperation with the Japanese.

The statement itself, after quite a review of the history of Jewish settlement in Manchuria, credits the Japanese with having curbed the anti-Jewish agitation of the White Russians. It calls attention to the fact that the Jewish flag flew side by side with the Manchurian and Japanese flags during the Far Eastern Conference. It reports with pride and joy that when the "Hatikvah" was played, as the song of the Jewish National Movement, Japanese and Manchurian officials stood at attention, and the Jews who observed this, were staunch in their own pride.

"Ever since then," the statement emphasizes, "we have been living a full national life. We send money to Palestine and publish our paper, *Jewish Life*. We take care of our poor and no restrictions have been placed against the refugees of Germany and Austria. In case of difficulties, a simple verbal declaration of the President of the Council in behalf of the refugees is enough for the authorities to permit these refugees to enter. The Jewish youth organization, B'rit Trumpeldor, had official colors and uniforms, and was excused from marching in a public parade in honor of Germany's recognition of Manchukuo. While other countries eventually granted citizenship to its new immigrants, legislation in Manchuria had not progressed that far. In the case of the Russian Jews, this meant that they lived in Manchuria without consular protection.

"But now the greater majority of the Jews were protected by the President of the Council, who carried no less weight in national affairs than any other consul of a great power. There was a limitless field for Jewish development in China. . . . Japan still remembered the financial help of Jacob Schiff. And when Prince Konoye, the Prime Minister, declared that Japan would not tolerate Communism or Fascism, the White Russian anti-Semites accused him of being a Jew."

In bold words, the report asserted that "Japan has no need for conferences to eliminate religious antagonism, as was the case in the United States. In Japan one could find, in one family and living respectfully side by side, Buddhists, Shintoists, Christians and members of other religions. And, finally, as to the question of how long Jews could remain in the Far East, the answer was forever, because Japan need not be considered an enemy of the Jews."

These were, indeed, strong words and assertions. They came at a time when the United States and England were doing all within their power to prevent the military growth and economic expansion of Japanese power in the Far East. In the United States, President Franklin D. Roosevelt, through a policy of moral embargo, was trying to slow the flow of strategic materials which would strengthen the Japanese war machine. The authors of the report must have been sharply aware of the anxiety in

Western circles over the ever-closer ties between Japan and Germany. They attempted to deal with this development in this fashion:

"There is a conflict of economic interests between Germany and Japan on the issue of China. Japan could expect nothing but competition from Germany and Italy and no financial assistance from them whatsoever. From the United States and England, however, Japan could expect financial help and comparatively no competition."

In conclusion, the statement recommended that the American Jewish leaders and their organizations publicly express their gratitude to Japan and their hope that Japan continue to aid the Jews living in Japanese-held territory.

Dr. Adler of the American Jewish Committee merely acknowledged the report. Dr. Wise of the American Jewish Congress, however, was outspoken against any Jewish support for "Fascist" Japan.

I think one may be permitted to speculate, to some extent, on the reactions and motives of these Jewish leaders; on the official silence of Dr. Adler and the sharp condemnation by Dr. Wise. It is possible that Dr. Adler deemed it expedient to remain silent in order to avoid any friction between Japan and Germany. A public statement praising the Japanese, coming from a Jewish spokesman, would possibly have led the Japanese to become less friendly to the Jews under her control or those refugees who had to pass through her territories. As for Dr. Wise, it can be assumed that he, too, had second thoughts about his adamant stand against the Japanese. When World War II broke out in 1939, the main escape routes in Europe were cut off in the Western part of the continent. The Trans-Siberian Railroad remained the only way out of the Hitler inferno. Dr. Wise then took a somewhat different position than he did in the past. In 1940, he no longer objected to plans for settling refugees in Manchuria, provided that such a proposal was made by re-

sponsible Japanese authorities and with the sanction of the
American State Department. Dr. Wise must have concluded that
it was not to the best interests of the Jewish people—nor was it
to the advantage of the United States—to lump Japan with Nazi
Germany.

We know now that the prestige and status of the National
Council and its Jewish leaders helped thousands of refugees
passing through Manchuria between 1939 and 1941. More: the
contacts between the Japanese and the Jewish leaders—made
prior to the outbreak of war between the United States and
Japan—continued to exert a restraining influence on the Japanese
at a time when Nazi pressure on Japan was most extreme.

The Third Far Eastern Conference

No official report exists on the second conference of 1938,
but there are two on the third conference, which took place on
December 23, 1939 and lasted four days. One report was made
by Kanichiro Kubota, Consul General of Harbin, and was dated
January 11, 1940. The other was made by Consul Shimomura
Suso, and was dated January 17, 1940.

In attendance at this conference were nineteen delegates
from Kobe, Tsingtao, Shanghai, Tientsin, Dairen, Mukden,
Chichihar, Hailar and Harbin. There was one main subject on
the agenda: how to deal with the problem of the 17,000 refugees
who had managed to reach Shanghai. The conference was attended by important Manchurian and Japanese officials, who
represented their governments and spoke briefly at the conference. Colonel Yasue also was among the speakers. According
to one of the reports available on the meeting, we learn that a
Dr. Kotsuji, a Hebrew scholar and advisor to the South Manchurian Railway Company, spoke in Hebrew and made a profound impression upon his audience of 800. A silent prayer was
offered at the conference to the memory of a Rev. Nakada, who

had died a few months previously. Rev. Nakada had fought hard
for the equality of races and had been a staunch battler against
anti-Semitism. He also promoted friendship between the Japanese and the Jews.

The Jewish delegates at the conference—as delegates do at
all conferences—adopted a series of resolutions and cabled the
texts of the resolutions to the Jewish organizations in New York,
London and Geneva. The conference had called for Japanese
and Manchurian authorities to provide jobs for the refugees and
to issue visas to them so that they could enter and leave Manchuria. The Jews promised to assist in the screening of the
refugees and they called for a number of other developments,
all of which would help make the Jewish community in the area
tighter and more effective and efficient.

The Japanese issued their own report and in it they expressed
their opinion that the participants in the conference were serious
in their plans to help the New Order in East Asia. They also
hoped that their policy of equal rights would attract American
capital and improve American-Japanese diplomatic relations.
They cautioned against allowing too many refugees to enter or
pass through Manchuria because they felt that too liberal a
policy might alienate the White Russians.

The National Council kept in touch with the Jewish communities of the Far East through mailing out circular letters in
which the Council suggested cultural and political programs. It
was suggested, for example, that the Jews mark the 2,600th
anniversary of the foundation of the Japanese Empire at synagogue services on February 11, 1940. At Tientsin Rabbi Kiseleff
and at Dairen Rabbi Levin preached on Japan's tolerance and
freedom from anti-Semitism in its long history. Special prayers
were offered for the welfare of His Majesty, the Emperor Tenno.

Such displays of friendship—and it is possible that they were,
in a sense, "command performances"—undoubtedly were influential in the maintenance of the security of the Jewish communities

in Manchuria and Japan. It may safely be stated that the behavior of the Jews also influenced the Japanese in their decent treatment of the Jews at a time when Japan's ally, Nazi Germany, had embarked on an extermination policy unequalled in world history for its sadism, its effectiveness and its brutality.

From time to time, Japanese officials and individuals made public statements in condemnation of the Nazi policy to wipe out the Jewish people. One of the observations should, however, be recorded here. It was made by Foreign Minister Matsuoka at a private dinner party in his Tokyo residence on December 31, 1940. He was speaking to a prominent Jewish businessman when he said, "I just want to assure you that anti-Semitism will never be adopted by Japan. True, I concluded a treaty with Hitler, but I never promised him to be an anti-Semite. And this is not only my personal opinion, but it is a principle of the entire Japanese empire since the day of its foundation." When the Foreign Minister was asked if his statement could be publicly quoted, he freely gave his consent.

Nevertheless, there remained some feelings of mutual distrust between Jew and Japanese. This suspicion grew in intensity during the years of 1941, 1942, 1943 and 1944, the era of close Japanese-German ties. While the Jewish population of Manchuria and China had no choice except to lend their support to the Japanese war effort, there is little reason to doubt that the Jews were pleased when the tides of war turned against the Japanese war machine. They were happy to see the crumbling of the Japanese alliance with their Nazi allies who were embarked not only on a war of conquest against the world but upon an unequal and violent war of annihilation against millions of Jews.

CHAPTER II

CHINA

IN ORDER TO UNDERSTAND the life and situation of the Jews in China, one must first have some awareness of the structure and political, social and communal pattern of life in Shanghai, the largest city of China. Only then can the reader fathom some of the mysteries of the so-called intriguing East and only then can the scholar of Jewish history realize why and how Jews behaved in this part of the world in a particular time and in a special place.

Much of the general historical material that follows is based on an important volume, *Shanghai: Key to Modern China*, written by Rhoads Murphey in 1953. Nevertheless, the reader should remember that the general material is offered here mainly to clarify the position of the Jews in this area.

Shanghai was opened to foreign trade more than one hundred years ago, in 1843. Because of its fortunate location, Shanghai developed at a phenomenal rate and in a period of one hundred years, it became one of the greatest import and export centers in the world. It is located near the Yangtze River delta, and its natural rivers are used as lanes for the flow of material into and out of China. As a result of this heavy trade, Shanghai became one of the leading financial centers of the world as well as a great port.

The city was especially attractive to the foreigner because of its principle of extra-territoriality, which placed citizens of foreign nationalities under the exclusive jurisdiction of their own countries. These legal rights gave foreigners special advantages in business dealings and helped secure their property and their very persons.

In time, this principle became a thorn in the side of the Chinese, who considered extra-territoriality a symptom of China's weakness and flabbiness. Eventually, these rights were yielded up by the powers that enjoyed them, even though this right helped raise Shanghai to previously unprecedented business levels.

There were three independent political units in Shanghai. There was the original Chinese group; and then there was the International Settlement and, finally, there was the French Concession, which contained most of the foreign residences.

There was another oddity about Shanghai. Although it was the center for Christian missionary efforts in China, it was far from a "clean" city. On the contrary, Shanghai enjoyed the reputation of being one of the most wicked cities in the world, where one could purchase almost anything, any vice, any drug, for money. Prostitution was rampant and opium was readily available. All this, in spite of the missionaries in the area.

The evil was abetted by the extra-territoriality, for the independent municipalities provided easy access to criminals and others for disappearing and avoiding extradition. Kidnapping was common in the city and, indeed, the very frequency of the practice gave the name of "Shanghaiing" to kidnapping. Crews for ships were easily obtained in this fashion. Foreigners and Chinese were "shanghaied" by roving gangs and the victims were used as coolie labor on East or West Indian plantations as well as on ships.

It is, therefore, easy to visualize the constant flux in the population. Few people came to the city with the expectation of staying for any length of time. Most wanted to make a quick fortune and leave the city. One of the results of this mood and atmosphere was that Shanghai was an exciting city, with an international flavor, with a mixing of cultures and with men and women from all parts of the world moving into and out of the international port.

In addition to the foreigners, Chinese refugees kept entering whenever there was trouble at home. And there was plenty of trouble, for there were constant local wars and battles between 1850 and 1950. Even the casual student will recall the Taiping Rebellion (1850–1864); the Franco-Chinese War (1884–1885); the Boxer Rebellion (1900); World War I; the Japanese attack on Shanghai in 1932 and the Japanese-Chinese War from 1937 to 1945. And these are only a handful of samples. Of course, we must also take into account the war between the Nationalists and the Communists, which led to a general exodus from Shanghai. But this deserves special treatment and will be dealt with in a later chapter.

The periodic influx of impoverished refugees provided a source of cheap labor for industry. Factory conditions and wage standards were as low as that of the Chinese. Housing, even in the slums, was extremely scarce and real estate was at a premium. It is obvious that, under these conditions, the public health situation was in a dangerous state. In 1935, for example, which was a comparatively peaceful year in China, the Shanghai Municipal Council collected 5,590 corpses—lying around the streets of the International Settlement. This does not take into account, the dead bodies picked up in the other locales. Two years later, in 1937, the figure came to 20,746!

With poor public health conditions, with miserable sanitary facilities, it was clear that the fear of epidemics was a valid fear, for from time to time the death rate rose alarmingly. The few attempts made to improve the situation were hampered by foreign and Chinese property owners, who felt they would lose money in the process. Money, according to Murphey, dominated Shanghai and everything else yielded to greed.

Technically, Shanghai was part of China and was Chinese soil. Yet the Chinese government was unable to collect any taxes, except for maritime customs dues and a land tax. The Shanghai Municipal Council had the exclusive right to tax the Chinese and foreigners within the settlement. What is more significant, all the foreign powers, who enjoyed their own particular treaty relations with China, claimed the right to land their own troops in the territory in order to protect their own citizens. The result was that no foreign settlement was ever invaded by a hostile force, until the Japanese occupied Shanghai after 1941.

In Murphey's *Shanghai: Key to Modern China,* there is a breakdown of the city's population and it is a most interesting analysis for those who would understand the role of the Jews in the city.

Between the two World Wars, Shanghai became a haven for both foreigners and Chinese. The first refugees who arrived were those who fled the Russian Revolution. Between 1919 and 1930, about 1,000 a year came into the city, and many of them were Jewish. The Jewish influx was even higher with the rise of Nazism in Germany and Austria. The unfortunate Jews, forced to tear up their roots in order to save their lives—and by now we know that only a comparative handful had the strength of character to do so—discovered that Shanghai was the only major port city prepared to accept them. Entry was not difficult and official residence, even if temporary, was easier to obtain in Shanghai than in other large harbor cities.

In 1936, for instance, there were about 60,000 foreigners in Shanghai. According to Murphey, there were 20,000 Japanese; 15,000 Russians, predominantly White Russians; 9,000 British subjects; 5,000 Germans and Austrians, mostly Jewish; 4,000 Americans and 2,500 Frenchmen.

The Jews of Shanghai

The Jews started to arrive in Shanghai in 1843, when the general influx of foreigners began. The intensive period of foreign settlement lasted about one hundred years and in that time there were three distinct phases of Jewish immigration and settlement. First, Shanghai accepted the Sephardic Jews, then the Russian Jews and finally the refugees from Hitler's Europe. This does not mean that Jews from other lands did not settle in Shanghai. They did, but not in large enough numbers to form their own communities. Some came from France, from Italy and even from the United States, but not enough to make a major impact on the communal patterns of the city.

Because Sephardic Jewry is distinguished and the history of these Jews important in the annals of the Jewish people, there have been many accounts written of the lives, history and achievement of the Sephardim. The literature on Sephardic Jewry is rich and some of the following information is culled from works by the noted historian Cecil Roth, from the *Jewish Encyclopedia* on Shanghai and from a volume by D. S. Sassoon entitled *A History of the Jews in Baghdad*.

Cecil Roth correctly calls attention to the fact that the role of the Sephardim in developing and influencing the East and Far East has not yet been fully and comprehensively described. In the nineteenth century, there was a heavy migration westward of German Jews. These people contributed to the development, financial and cultural, of France and the English-speaking countries. A prime and exciting example of German-Jewish influence and power was the House of Rothschild, international bankers who played a key role in the economic and commercial development of the Western world.

At about this same time, there was a similar movement in

the reverse direction. Between 1820 and 1914, Jews from Meso-
potamia and Baghdad moved—constantly, but on a smaller
scale—to the East and the Far East. A fabulous Jewish family,
the Sassoons, dominated this era. This family was instrumental
in establishing, indeed, creating, new communities in India, on
the Malay Peninsula, and then in China. In Shanghai, around
1850, Elias David Sassoon opened a branch office in affiliation
with his father's commerical and trading establishment in Bom-
bay, India. This led to a steady flow of clerks and their families
to Shanghai, connected, at the outset, with the Sassoon firm and
the various branches of the organization. Later, however, many
of these people established their own independent firms, and
in this fashion, the Far East was peopled with Westerners.

In 1860, the Sassoons established a cemetery in Shanghai. A
few years later, the Elias family started another cemetery. It was
clear that there were many Jews in the city by this time—and
where cemeteries exist, there is eloquent testimony to the fact
that people live and die in a given area.

Up until 1898, the Jews worshipped in a small hall, but it
proved to be inadequate. Eventually a small synagogue, Shearit
Israel, was built on Seward Road and dedicated by D. E. J.
Abraham. In 1905, a second synagogue was erected. It was called
Beth El. These synagogues served the religious needs of the
entire Jewish community which, at the beginning of the twenti-
eth century, numbered 600 souls, nearly all of them Sephardim
from the Mediterranean and Oriental areas of the world.

But there must have been a small group of Ashkenazim as
well, Jews from the countries of Europe, for in 1905, these people
rented a hall of their own for the High Holidays. This is an
interesting phenomenon, one which occurred again and again:
where Sephardim and Ashkenazim existed side by side, developing their own traditions according to their own view of Judaism
and following in the footsteps and customs of their fathers. Grad-

ually, too, they started to blend and work together in areas of mutual concern and interest.

The strong position of the British Empire in the Far East deeply influenced the political and social outlook of the Sephardic Jewish community. In 1898, for example, Sephardic Jews already had established a branch of the Anglo-Jewish Association and many of the families, individually, were British subjects.

It is worth noting, on the other hand, that some Jews in the Far East did not maintain their ties with the Jewish people overseas. The Chinese Jews of Kai-Feng-Fu (a fascinating group of people worth a complete study on their own) were totally integrated into the Chinese population and a 1900 attempt to organize these Jews and to create an aid society with their aid and for their benefit (by E. M. Ezra) failed. It was, by this time, too late to keep the Chinese Jews within the larger world Jewish community.

The Shanghai Jewish community was sufficiently well organized for these Jews to be represented at the sixth Zionist Congress at Basle, Switzerland in 1903. By 1905, the Sephardim had organized a Talmud Torah and a secular school—all this when the group had a maximum of 700 persons. Thus, it is to the credit of the leading Sephardic families that they established two beautiful synagogues in the heart of the foreign settlement. The first one, Ohel Rachel, was erected in 1922 by Sir Jacob Sassoon in his wife's memory. Five years later, S. A. Hardoon, built Beth Aharon in his father's memory.

It was in Beth Aharon that 300 students of the Mir Yeshiva continued their studies during World War II, at a time when housing was extremely difficult to obtain.

One of the outstanding Jewish leaders of this community was N. E. B. Ezra, the founder and editor of *Israel's Messenger*, a magazine that flourished in Shanghai from 1904 to 1941, except for the years 1910–1918. It was a well-edited and influential

monthly Jewish journal and reflected accurately the life of the
Jews in Shanghai during critical and significant years.

One of the most important achievements of Ezra was a letter
he received, in support of the Zionist movement, from Dr. Sun
Yat-sen, the founder of modern China. Because of the historic
importance of this letter, I quote it in full:

> Dr. Mr. Ezra:
> I have read your letter and the copy of *Israel's Messen-
> ger* with much interest, and wish to assure you of my sym-
> pathy for this movement—which is one of the greatest
> movements of the present time. All lovers of Democracy
> cannot help but support the movement to restore your
> wonderful and historic nation, which has contributed so
> much to the civilization of the world and which rightfully
> deserves an honourable place in the family of nations.
>
> > I am
> > Yours very truly,
> > Sun Yat-sen
>
> 29 Rue Molière
> 24 April 1920

The sentiments in this letter were endorsed in 1947 by Sun
Fo, the son of Dr. Sun Yat-sen, in a letter to Miss Judith Hasser
of the Zionist-Revisionist movement in Shanghai.

Ezra's work was deeply appreciated by the Jews of the Far
East and he worked indefatigably in behalf of the Jews of Harbin. He died in 1936 and his magazine was continued under
the guidance of his widow. This increasingly important publication called itself "a fearless exponent of Traditional Judaism and
Jewish Nationalism." It also served as the "official organ of the
Shanghai Zionist Association and the Jewish National Fund
Commission for China." Unfortunately, there does not exist in
the United States a complete set of this monthly journal. The
most complete collection (April 1904–April 1905; April 1936–
July 1941) is to be found in the New York Public Library at
42nd Street in the archives of the Jewish Division.

The Russian Jews

After the Russo-Japanese War of 1904–1905, a group of Russian Jews found their way to Shanghai and formed the first Ashkenazic congregation, Ohel Moshe, in 1907. The synagogue was named after Moshe Greenberg, an early settler. I am grateful to Manfred Rosenfeld for much of the foregoing material, which is based on Mr. Rosenfeld's unpublished manuscript on "The History of the Shanghai Jewish Communities," which is to be found in the YIVO archives in New York City.

The Russian Jewish community expanded following the 1917 Russian revolution and by the mid-1920's, there were more Russian Jews in Shanghai than there were Sephardim. In the 1930's, more Russian Jews arrived from Manchuria and Harbin. By 1932, the community had grown so large that a new synagogue had to be built and an official Ashkenazi community was founded under the name of Hakehilla Haivrith Ha'Ashkenazith.

The synagogue itself, at 26 Ward Road, soon proved to be too small for the community and was eventually replaced by a spacious edifice, dedicated in 1941 at 102 Rue de la Tour in the French Concession, where most of the Russian Jews lived. The Shanghai Ashkenazic Jewish Communal Association, established in 1932, originally consisted of Russian Jews only, but later included Jews from Poland. This association officially represented the Ashkenazic Jews. Its meetings were conducted in the Russian language and between 1943 and 1945, the majority of the Russian Jews (1000 families or 4000 persons) were registered in the association.

The Russian Jews earned their living as businessmen working, in the main, at the export-import trade, and as small shopkeepers. They were not as prosperous as some of the earlier Sephardic settlers, yet they managed to make out well and to establish a firm economic base in Shanghai. In 1937, they won official recognition through registration with the Shanghai Municipal Council.

The spiritual leader of this ever-growing and developing unit was Rabbi Meir Ashkenazi, who had arrived in Shanghai in the 1920's, after having lived in Vladivostok and Harbin. The rabbi, who was a Lubavitcher chassid, a member of an extremely pious and famed chassidic sect, wielded much influence in the community and was universally admired for his goodness of heart, for his piety and for his constant willingness to help his brother Jews in trouble. Unhappily, he was not a healthy man—having expended his energies during the terrible years of 1941–1945, and was unable to achieve all that he might have achieved had he been sturdy and less frail. He died in New York City in 1956.

The Russian Jews, like all other Jews in other lands and climes, quickly established institutions for their people. The first communal institution was the Shelterhouse for the Aged, which had a large dining room whose facilities were available to all those who were in need. Some 400 hot meals were served daily from the kitchen. This shelterhouse took on particular significance during World War II, because employees of foreign firms suddenly found themselves without work, due to the dislocations of the war, and needed help. In addition, those who still had jobs were earning small salaries and could not afford to eat in restaurants. Nevertheless, because many of those in need were reluctant to enter the shelterhouse itself, the community organized a restaurant, where good food was served at low prices.

Another important institution established by this group was the Jewish Club. In 1931, it was established in modest, rented premises. But the club soon outgrew the space it had and found a second and a third building were still inadequate. Eventually, the club acquired new facilities, which formerly housed the United States Navy Club. After Pearl Harbor, in late 1941, this edifice was occupied by the Japanese authorities and the club moved to the local Masonic building, and it remained there throughout the war.

The club was operated separately and independently of the synagogue. All of the social life of the Russian Jews centered around this club, which was, in effect, a home to many of them. Many Jews met at the club not only for social events but for communal meetings as well. Among the club features were musical concerts, lectures and plays staged by theatrical groups in the vicinity. The cultural life of the community was on a high standard because the White Russian community boasted many fine artists in Shanghai. The result was that there was in town a fine ballet company, an excellent symphony orchestra, and light and classical opera companies. The Jews of Shanghai flocked to the many cultural activities and the club was, thus, the heart of the community's social life.

But this was not the end of organized Jewish life among the Russian Jews of Shanghai. They established a Talmud Torah, a Free Loan Society, which had more than 400 members, a Chevra Kadisha (a burial society) and a weekly newspaper, published in Yiddish and in Russian.

While the religious and social institutions of the Ashkenazic community were developed separately from those of the Sephardim, there were certain areas where they came together.

One of these areas centered about the Jewish school which was established in 1930 thanks to the legacy of I. S. Perry of Hong Kong, plus the contributions of the local community. Mr. Perry's legacy stipulated that the $150,000 he was leaving for the school had to be matched by the community itself before his money could be used. It was a model school, well-built and well-planned. Up until 1941, it was operated by the trustees of the Sephardic community. Later, the Ashkenazic Jews became responsible for running the school because most of the Sephardic Jews—who had retained their British citizenship—had been interned by the Japanese.

During the years of the Japanese occupation of Shanghai, this Jewish school assumed special status and importance, for most of the other foreign schools deteriorated badly or had to be shut down for lack of enough teachers. Until the war, many Jewish parents had sent their children to the municipal English public schools in the International Settlement or to schools within the French Concessions. Like all English schools, the Jewish school was based on the British educational system. Upon graduation, students received the London Cambridge Matriculation Certificate, which was a highly desirable certificate. Those parents unable to afford the tuition fees at the Jewish school were offered free education for their children.

Shanghai had two universities where foreign students could obtain a higher education. One was St. John's University, which was supported and organized and operated by American Episcopalian missionaries. The second was Aurora, a French university under Jesuit direction and control. Few Jewish children, however, continued their education in Shanghai itself before the war. Usually, they were sent to the United States. During the war, about twenty were graduated from St. John's and Aurora, of whom three were refugees from Hitler Europe.

Another Jewish institution within the Russian Jewish community was the local B'nai B'rith Lodge which involved itself in many charitable works. It sponsored a medical clinic which later developed into the Jewish hospital and it provided medical care to persons of many nationalities. It was well-administered and excellently-staffed. In time, it became self-supporting.

In describing the various Jewish institutions and organizations in Shanghai, one cannot omit a most important group, the Jewish Company, which was organized in the early 1930's and was part of the Shanghai Volunteer Corps. This corps is not too easy to define. It was created in order to protect the foreign settlement against internal and external disturbances. It was a sort of fire brigade, but it did not fight fires as such. It fought against human disturbers. It was, in a sense, the first international police force and served its purposes very well for a time. Some 200 to 250 Jews made up the Jewish Company and they were commanded by a Jewish captain. It afforded the Jews an opportunity to shoulder some of the necessary civic responsibilities—but as an organized Jewish unit. It gave the Jews status and recognition and it helped raise the morale of both the Sephardic and Ashkenazic communities of the city of Shanghai.

The Refugees and Japan's New Order

It is most difficult to recount the story of the refugees who lived in Shanghai. They constituted the third—and largest—element of Shanghai's Jewry. This was an emotion-laden era—the years between 1937 and 1945—and there are many points of view to be considered in telling how the refugees lived under the Japanese occupation and during the years when Japan imposed its New Order upon the people living in the territories under Japanese control.

Before any accurate and correct account can be undertaken, the reader must first set into focus the overall picture. It has to be remembered that it was during these years that Japan's power expanded into an area in which there lived more than 130,000,000 people. Japan conceived of a new sphere of what is called Co-Prosperity, with a large family of nations with Japan as its head. Japan challenged the rights of the Western nations in the Far East, those very Western Powers which had carefully developed their own spheres of influence and power in the Far East, after many years of laborious work and effort.

The Japanese operated under the slogan "Asia for the Asiatics," but, simultaneously, Japan attempted to increase its power over Manchuria and North China. This effort finally led to the war between China and Japan in July, 1937.

The New Order was vigorously pursued by the Japanese mil-

itarists who, since 1931, had consistently increased their influence
and control over Japanese politics. Shanghai, it is well to remember, was the center and the stronghold of the Western democ-
racies in China. Thus, this great port was a special target of
the Japanese.

The Japanese were not strangers in this city. The fact is that
by 1937, there were 20,000 Japanese in Shanghai among the
60,000 foreigners in the city. Like the other Treaty Powers,
Japan maintained a naval force of some 2,000 men for the
protection of her nationals and commercial interests. This force,
called the Naval Landing Party, held the Hongkow and Yangtze-
poo areas of the International Settlement and a section of North
Hongkew.

As a result of a local incident, Chinese and Japanese forces
met in battle at Shanghai on August 13, 1937. When the Japanese government realized that its troops were heavily outnum-
bered by the Chinese, the Japanese sent army units into the
Shanghai area, asserting at the same time that their only intention was to chastise the lawless Chinese. The Japanese denied
that they had any territorial designs on China and declared that
they would continue to respect the right and interests of the
foreign powers.

In spite of these protestations and declarations, the Japanese
nevertheless attempted to gain control of most of the International Settlement in Shanghai. On January 4, 1938, the Japanese
military and consular authorities demanded that the Municipal
Council of the International Settlement (composed, in 1931, of
five British, two American, two Japanese and five Chinese members) appoint Japanese subjects to key positions in all branches
of the local administration. They also insisted that more Japanese be placed in the Settlement police force and asked for
control of Sectors B and D of the Settlement, hitherto garrisoned
by the British. On this final request, the Japanese were turned
down, for Sector B comprised the heart of the Settlement. In-

stead, the area was taken over by the Shanghai Volunteer Corps, and was held by this unit until the outbreak of war between Japan and the United States. Only then did the Japanese win control of the entire city.

This was the tense local situation, fraught with peril, when some 20,000 Jewish refugees began to pour into the city in August, 1938. This influx lasted for a full year, until August, 1939, shortly before the outbreak of World War II in Europe. The fact that the newcomers were Jews did nothing to irritate or aggravate the already-explosive situation. To the average Japanese—as well as to the Chinese—the term "Jew" and the concept of the Jewish religion were of little significance. Anti-Semitism, as it is known and accepted in the Western world, was practically unknown in Japan. The Jew was merely another foreigner who, during the period of Japanese domination, simply had to fall into line, like the other foreigners.

It is interesting to note that the word "Jew" does not appear at all in the more than 160 volumes of the International Military Tribunal of the Far East, which contain the record of the charges of the Western Allies against the important prisoners in the Far East. Yet it is stated by the Japanese historian Kobayashi that "It may be said that it was a mistake of the International Military Tribunal not to take up the Japanese type of anti-Semitism, which exerted a great and vicious influence on the thinking of many."

The question of Japanese anti-Semitism, even if it did not exist in the form recognizable to us, is not uncomplicated. Anti-Jewish bias was introduced to the Japanese officers when they became acquainted with White Russians in Siberia and Manchuria after the Russian revolution. Some of these White Russians disseminated propaganda which stressed that "Jews are Communists" and were responsible for the misery and the exile of the White Russians.

I believe that in any discussion of Japanese anti-Semitism,

one must carefully make the distinction between what the Japanese military leaders came to believe and the kind of anti-Semitism practiced by the Nazis or other European peoples. Anti-Semitism in the Far East was the intellectual property of a handful of misguided individuals. According to Kobayashi, the problem of the Jew was debated as early as 1921 in various Japanese periodicals and in some meeting halls.

The vicious *Protocols of the Elders of Zion*, and other anti-Jewish material, was translated into Japanese. According to Kobayashi, the first translation into Japanese of the Protocols was made in 1919 by Tsu yanosuke Higuchi, in his volume *The Essence of Bolshevism*. The author had lived in Russia before World War I and taught Russian in the Japanese Army and served as an interpreter as well. He wrote under the penname of Baiseki Kitagami. His book was published secretly in Siberia.

A detailed study of Japanese anti-Semitic literature has yet to be made. The Library of Congress in Washington, D.C., has in its possession some thirty titles in the Japanese language on Jews and the Jewish problem. Almost all of these pamphlets and brochures and articles were published in the 1930's and 1940's. In addition, there were two important projects on the Jews which deserve to be mentioned at this juncture.

The first one is *Koksai himitsuryoku no Kenkyu* (Studies in the International Conspiracy), an annual which appeared in six volumes from 1936–1940. These studies were continued by *Yudaya Kenkyu* (Studies on the Jews) a monthly journal which appeared in three volumes, from May 1941 to June 1943. It has been assumed that the magazine was forced to discontinue publication two years before the end of the war because of a shortage of funds.

Much of this material and literature has been carefully analyzed and summarized by Dr. Rudolph Loewenthal in an unpublished manuscript on "Japanese and Chinese Materials on the Jewish Catastrophe of 1939–45."

On the basis of what is known of Japanese policy toward the Jews, it can be stated that these journals and annuals and the material contained in them cannot be connected with official Japanese policy. In 1939, Foreign Minister Arita declared in the Japanese Diet that there was no legal reason to segregate the Jewish communities in Japan. It must also be recalled that in Manchuria and in North China the Jews enjoyed equal rights with other groups. On the other hand, we cannot overlook the lugubrious fact that after the outbreak of the war in the East, these anti-Semitic journals and magazines exercised considerable influence on the members of the Kempeitai, the secret military police in China, and upon the authorities of the Japanese puppet state of Manchukuo. We must bear in mind that much of the official Japanese policy was made and executed by the local military and civilian authorities—which explains, in some measure, the wide range of policy and behavior toward the Jews.

Some of the contributors to these anti-Jewish journals were highly-placed Japanese government officials and military intelligence officers. I think that if I were to introduce one of them and describe his background and career, we may obtain a good insight into the mentality of the Japanese of that era and to understand the problems of the Jews in that time and place. The officer I have in mind is Colonel Sanko Yasue, and I believe that it will be instructive to devote some space to him as a person and as a leader.

Colonel Senko Yasue

In order to draw an historically accurate portrait of this Japanese officer, I have had the benefit of the cooperation of the colonel's son, who supplied me with detailed information on the life of his father. But the son apparently was unaware of his father's attitude toward the Jews. The historian Kobayashi, after examining the material I obtained, observed that "concerning one

aspect of his father's career, as an anti-Semitic writer and researcher, the son seems to be completely ignorant."

The colonel's son does admit that his father, Colonel Norihiro
(Senko) Yasue, was familiar with the Protocols, even though
the colonel was well-known and respected among the Jews of
the Far East. Colonel Yasue was an Army officer who devoted
much of his military career to the study of Jewish history and
the so-called "Jewish" problem. He was born in 1888 of a
Samurai family and after he received his education as a cadet,
he became a Russian linguist and taught at the Tokyo School
for Foreign Languages. He served with the Japanese army in its
Siberian expedition and worked closely with White Russian
elements. It was through his White Russian contacts that Colonel
Yasue became aware of and interested in Jews.

Eventually, his studies came to the attention of General
Shirakawa, who recommended that Yasue—then a Major—be
made the army's specialist on the history of the Jews. Thus,
the Japanese colonel became a Jewish expert.

Before I discuss his career in greater detail, I should like to
make a few points on the basis of the observations of Kobayashi.
Here are some of Kobayashi's comments:

"Yasue himself was among the earliest translators of the
Protocols in Japan. The main part of Yasue's *Inside the World
Revolution* was a translation of the Protocols. This book appeared under his penname, Hokoshi. Information as to his penname came from General Nobutaka Shioden."

Kobayashi also stated that General Shioden, a leader in the
field of Japanese aviation, stood for election to the House of
Representatives in 1942 with the avowed aim to shut out the
"international secret power," meaning the Jews. He was one of
the principal anti-Semitic leaders of Japan.

The reader will remember that Yasue was respected by the
Jewish community and Kobayashi believes that this mistaken
opinion was due primarily to the Jewish lack of knowledge of

the Japanese language and the anti-Semitic literature that was published in that tongue.

I am reluctant to accept this reason as the full explanation. When I presented Kobayashi's information on Yasue to the Jews who knew him, they found it impossible to believe that he was anti-Jewish. They remembered his friendship with the Jewish leaders of the era. They knew his name had been entered in the Golden Book of the Jewish National Fund and they recalled his active help to Jewish refugees during 1938, 1939 and 1940, when he served as chief of the Military Mission in Dairen, during which period he also was liaison officer to the Far Eastern Jewish Council.

It is possible to suggest the following: that Yasue was a Japanese patriot who, in his earlier years, actually believed the Jews to be a "secret world power." As late as 1936, he said in his published writings that while Zionism seems to be the aim of the Jews, that is, the establishment of a Jewish homeland in Palestine, the Jews actually want to control the whole world. Later, when he faced up to the influx of refugees from Nazism, he was guided by his innate humanitarian impulses and his patriotism. Therefore, he resented the Nazi policies against the Jews and the close alliance between Germany and his own country. By helping the Jews, Yasue might have felt that he could improve Japan's position in the world.

Yasue's son insists that his father sympathized with the Jewish people and that he did not like to be called "pro-Jewish." He preferred to be known as a humanitarian. It seemed at this time that Yasue—when he was friendly with Jews—was not precisely following the pattern of thought of the Japanese army and so he faced the repeated risk of being ousted from the military service. He was placed as an instructor in the Tokyo Dental College from 1930 to 1937 and then, during the outbreak of war with China, was sent to Dairen as the chief of the Military Mission. In the summer of 1939, Colonel Yasue spent much time in

Shanghai as the army member of the local Japanese Investigation Committee which had been organized in order to cope with the influx of refugees from Europe. But there is an interesting aside to be mentioned here. According to Yasue's son, the colonel had been dismissed from his post in Dairen by War Minister Tojo because the colonel had anti-Nazi attitudes. Tojo offered to reinstate Yasue if he would cooperate with the pro-Nazi policies of the Tojo government. He refused and during his retirement served as advisor to the South Manchuria Railway Company in Dairen until 1945. He was placed under military police surveillance during the war and was arrested in 1945 by the Russians. He died in a Soviet prison in the summer of 1950. Representatives of the Jewish community attended the memorial services in his honor which were held in Tokyo.

This, then, is the tale of a single Japanese officer deeply involved in Jewish matters. It is a confusing story, without too much logic and full of bewilderment. Perhaps this is typical of the entire Jewish situation in the Far East.

Japanese Attitudes Toward Jews

It is known that there existed in Tokyo a "Moslem and Jewish Problem Committee," whose aim it was to debate and discuss various issues connected with Moslem and Jewish elements under Japanese control. Members of this committee included representatives of the army, the navy and the foreign office. This unit advised the government and local Shanghai authorities and elsewhere in China as to the policies and measures to be adopted in relation to refugee problems.

Three main groups represented the interested parties. There were the authorities of the Shanghai Municipal Council, which was (until Pearl Harbor) the administrative body of the foreign Settlement. Second, there were the Japanese military and consular authorities which (up to Pearl Harbor) controlled one sector of the Settlement through the Naval Landing Party and (after Pearl Harbor) later controlled the entire city. Third, there were the Jews themselves.

The Jewish group has to be divided, too, into two major components: resident Jews, and those who came in as refugees after 1937. In turn, the resident Jews were divided into two separate groups, the Sephardim and the Ashkenazim. The Sephardim were more affluent and pro-British. The Ashkenazim were not as well-established as the Sephardim and were, in the main, stateless Jews. The refugees who arrived in the area after 1937 were also divided. Thus, the interplay of forces complicated the political and the communal situation.

The Japanese viewpoint was expressed in a speech by Captain Kore-shige Inuzuka, a member of the Japanese Investigation Committee. Captain Inuzuka told the members of the Standing Committee of the "Moslem and Jewish Problem Committee" (on October 12, 1938) that the Japanese policies were based on the fact that the Japanese planned to establish a New Order in Asia and expected to mobilize all of their resources to promote this New Order.

The captain firmly believed that the Sephardic Jews were particularly interested in the Japanese attitude toward the refugees. He advocated that these Jews be cultivated, but at the same time suggested that his people should not become too friendly with them. "The local anti-Japanese Jews," he said, "must be strangled by the throat and subjected to complete oppression; they must be convinced of the necessity of depending upon the Japanese." He advocated that the official authorities should not contact the Jews, but that contact with them should be made by businessmen well briefed on the Jewish problem. Otherwise, he stated, the Jews may be led to believe that Japan was in financial difficulties.

Captain Inuzuka urged that a coordinated policy be established in which the Jews would not be denounced but their economic power in China would be exploited. He recommended that the Economic League of Japan establish a committee to study the Jewish problem and that this committee keep in close touch with the government. He also asked for better cooperation among the Japanese units in Shanghai, which included a branch of the International Institute of Politics and Economics; the Intelligence Services and the army and navy; the Consul General and the Shanghai branch of the Manchurian Railroad Company.

In conclusion, Captain Inuzuka said that the Jewish leaders in the area, who had heavy financial interests in Shanghai, were apparently becoming more sympathetic to Japan and less friendly to Great Britain. Since Japan needed more sums of money for the development of China, Captain Inuzuka declared it was important that the Japanese study in detail the methods whereby they could make use of the Jewish people.

The influx of the Jewish refugees also bothered Cornell S. Franklin, chairman of the Shanghai Municipal Council. In a letter dated December 23, 1938 to Dr. A. J. Alves, the Portuguese Consul General, Franklin stated that it was the Consul's duty to protect the community of the International Settlement by taking steps to prohibit the landing in the International Settlement of any further Jewish refugees without adequate means of subsistence or promise of employment.

While the refugee influx created a local problem for the Municipal Council, the Japanese were also greatly concerned with what they considered the problem of Jewish refugees in Japan, Manchukuo and China. On January 18, 1939, Mr. Kumabe, Chief of Section 3, American Bureau, reported on his investigation at a meeting of the "Moslem and Jewish Problem Committee." It was his mission to examine the problem created by the refugees in these areas of Japanese interest. He discovered that it was difficult for the Japanese to control the entry of Jews in Shanghai because the landing piers, which belong to foreigners, were not under the jurisdiction of the Municipal

Council. He pointed out that public opinion was in favor of checking the flow of refugees, in view of the 800,000 Chinese refugees who already were in Shanghai. Nevertheless, he was concerned that any measure of control undertaken by the Municipal Council might be interpreted as Japanese influence rather than local Shanghai influence.

Generally speaking, it was in Japan's interest to establish rigid control over foreign or Chinese Communists and anti-Japanese elements. It was important for the Japanese to check the Chinese entering the Garden Bridge, which was one of the main approaches to the Japanese-controlled areas of the International Settlement. But it was even more important that the highways be watched so that the Japanese could keep out Communist elements. Furthermore, since it was very difficult to maintain any stringent control within the Settlement itself, it was vital that shipping in and out of the ports of Shanghai and Tientsin be watched. Kumabe also urged that the Japanese should keep close watch over Tsingtao, Dairen and Peking. He advocated that the Japanese handle the refugees in Manchuria and North China with the cooperation of the Jewish communities there. This statement demonstrates the confidence the Japanese had in the Jewish communities organized through the Far Eastern Conference.

Kumabe felt that the situation was well in hand in Manchukuo, because here no foreigners were permitted to enter unless they had visas. He urged that Manchuria policy towards the Jews be patterned according to Japanese own policy and that the Legation of Manchuria in Berlin take action to check the flow of refugees.

As a result of the Tokyo meetings of the "Moslem and Jewish Problem Committee" an "On-the-Spot Committee" was formed to investigate Jewish problems in Shanghai. The members of this unit were Colonel Senko Yasue, Navy Captain Kore-Shigi Inuzuka and Consul Shiro Ishiguro. This group met on May 25,

1939 with Sir Victor Sassoon and Mr. Hayim, who represented the Committee for Assistance to European Refugees, known as COMAR.

In their own report on these discussions, the Japanese revealed that COMAR had a serious shortage of funds and that the Japanese themselves had tried to stop, through petitions of foreign consuls to Germany the flow of refugees into Shanghai. The Japanese group felt that it was now up to Japan to negotiate directly with Germany on the refugee problem, for some 12,000 refugees were depending, either partially or totally on relief. This relief was made possible with the aid of local government and non-governmental agencies of authorized countries.

One of the main reasons for the difficulties was the fact that refugees came in without funds. It was suggested that negotiations be initiated between Manchuria and Germany so that payment for care be made, in some fashion, with funds from Jewish property confiscated by the German government. Manchuria wanted merchandise rather than money and it was believed that goods would be easy to obtain since Manchuria had an agreement with Germany to pay for merchandise, in part, in sterling. Thus, Manchuria could buy the merchandise half in sterling (to Germany) and half in yen (to the refugees). An arrangement of this sort would also be convenient for Japan.

The Japanese authorities were asked by the COMAR representatives to help provide a warehouse, a school building—any kind of edifice—to serve as a shelter for the Jews in the area north of Shanghai. They were informed that there were no facilities available. The few buildings that were of some possible use were in such a state of disrepair that even if the Jews wanted to use them, they did not have the funds to make the buildings inhabitable.

According to the report, Sir Victor Sassoon is quoted as being grateful to the Japanese for being friendly to the Jews and for permitting Jews to enter Japanese territory.

The results of the meeting were reported to the Japanese Foreign Office by the Consul General and detailed plans were promised forthwith. Colonel Yasue, on behalf of the army, and Captain Inuzuka, representing the navy, submitted separate plans to their respective headquarters. There was then a Joint Committee report, written by Consul Ishiguro of the Foreign Office. The ultimate objective of all the plans, no matter who wrote them, was to control the flow of refugees into the Japanese-held and occupied territories.

It is worth noting that the Army and the Navy differed considerably in their approach to the problem. The Army's plan was more humane; the Navy's more direct and harsher.

The army report begins as follows: "The Japanese army, according to the national concept of the 'Eight Corners of the World Under One Roof,' will not refuse entry of Jewish refugees into Shanghai, but will try to avoid rapid increases in their numbers."

The interesting phrase of "Eight Corners of the World Under One Roof" represents a universalistic idea of brotherhood used by the Japanese in their desire to give a spiritual base to their policy of expansion.

The army plan advocated the temporary suspension of the entry of Jews into Shanghai. It pointed out that the severe shortage of building space in the city made it necessary to impose restrictions against Jews living in the city or engaging in business there. The Jewish Relief Committee was to make a survey of the Jewish population and the local police were to investigate all Jewish commercial establishments in the Hongkew area.

The plan also makes reference to the need to keep the area sanitary in order to prevent the spread of various diseases and pestilence, and the report stresses that at the moment of writing there were 350 refugees with scarlet fever. No details are too small for the army people to think about. Suggestions are given as to where new locations for the refugees should be. New

Shanghai, Pootung, Tsungming-Tao and Hainsntao are mentioned as being suitable places for the refugees to live.

Throughout, the army people emphasize that the refugees should be decently treated. It would be good for public opinion; it would ease the loan and investment situation; it would win the cooperation of the Jewish people in the Far East. The army plan takes into account the significance of Japan's "sacred war" and observes that "if we should take one false step, tens of thousands of souls of the dead and billions of yen, spent on the foundation of a New East Asia, would have been wasted."

The navy plan, on the other hand, was far less concerned with Japan's "historical mission." The navy report stresses the need of "enforcing a registration system" for the refugees. For example, all Jewish refugees residing within the district north of Soochow Creek had to be registered and those who already had been settled now had to be resettled in a camp operated by COMAR. Anybody living in the authorized sections or engaging in business without permission would be ordered out.

This harsh relocation plan, relating to those who already had been settled in Japanese-controlled areas, was not acceptable to the top Japanese authorities. Still, on the basis of emergency measures announced on July 1, 1939, no new refugees were to be allowed entry, except for those who already were on the high seas bound for Shanghai.

The joint report of the "on the spot" committee, was published on July 7, 1939. This report was designed to work out a Japanese policy for Jewish refugees and it also gave a historical survey of the various elements which constituted the local Jewish population. Mention is made of 4,000 Ashkenazim and 500 Sephardim. It stresses that the Ashkenazim favor Japan and that the Sephardim, originally pro-British, were caught in a conflict of interests between Great Britain and Japan. It analyzes the composition of the German refugees and the attitudes of the resident Jews toward the German refugees, some of whom were not

Jewish by religion, but Jewish by definition of the Nazi Nurem-
berg Laws. A handful of the refugees were Christians. Thus,
according to the report, "the local Jewish people cannot be quite
open-hearted toward the refugees who, though Jewish-blooded,
have much of German coloring and therefore are not always
agreeable to the British or Russian Jews."

Concerning the feelings of the "British Jews," the report
expresses the belief that such Jews were concentrated among
the upper classes or within the influential financial circles. The
other Jews were turning anti-English because of Britain's policies
in regard to Palestine. Instead, these Jews were turning to the
United States which, the report asserts, "was not a bad development as long as the United States remained neutral towards
Japan." The report also states that it was important that propaganda be increased, to persuade the Jews of Japan's strength.

Few angles are overlooked by the Japanese. They call attention to the fact that the Sassoons and other wealthy Jews
throughout the world could possibly be induced to help Japan in
building up the New China. An entire section is devoted to the
American scene and the President of the United States who "is
elected with the aid of the capitalists and whose position depends upon their support. Therefore, the policies of the country
are at the mercy of the capitalists, and eighty per cent of the
capitalists are Jewish."

This is one far-fetched statement. There are other gems of
illogic and wishful thinking. Here are a few passages culled from
the report which indicate the errors of the Japanese:

"The United States is a country of public opinion, and the
journalism which leads public opinion is again eighty per cent
Jewish, being under the influence of the Jewish financial
cliques."

"The inducement of Jewish capital is important at the present
time, but if we succeed in inducing American Jewish capital,
it will not only be worth while for financial purposes alone, but

the trust of American Jewish capitalists' trust in Japan will be strengthened."

"Our measures on the problem of the refugees in Shanghai shall clearly reflect our fair and sympathetic attitude and we will implant a sense of trust in Japan on the part of those who are now in international difficulties."

Quite apart from these curious observations, the report concludes with some practical suggestions. It asks for the establishment of an independent Jewish agency for the handling of refugees. There is stress on independence because "if this agency should be subordinated to the local military or civilian authorities, it is feared that it would not retain an over-all viewpoint. The Jewish operations, while directed primarily at Shanghai, must also include Japan, Manchuria, North China and other areas as well."

There is no doubt that the authors of this report were influenced by anti-Semitic material obtained by the Japanese "experts" on the "Jewish problem." These specialists were, it is obvious, serious about their task. And they were hopeful that their recommendations would help advance the position of the Japanese in Asia.

To demonstrate their seriousness, one can call attention to the Kogan Papers, unpublished material based on official Japanese documents hitherto unknown. The Kogan Papers include an "Estimate of Space Required for the Settlement of Jewish Refugees." This was prepared in May, 1940 by an official of the Special Investigating Section and was widely distributed to the authorized agencies dealing with the Jews. It was assumed that the Jewish population, at that time 20,000, would increase to between 30,000 and 70,000 within ten to twenty years.

All of these plans were fully aired by leaders and members of the "Moslem and Jewish Problem Committee" which met at Toyko in July, 1939. Following the deliberations of the Japanese experts on August 10, 1939, official consular action was taken.

Y. Miura, the Consul General of Japan in Shanghai, called attention to the fact that 5,000 refugees in the Japanese sector of Shanghai were causing some serious problems. He made this point in letters to Dr. E. Bracklo, Acting Consul General for Germany in Shanghai, and to Dr. F. Farinacci, Acting Consul General for Italy. In these letters, Miura urged the consuls to do what they could to halt the flow of refugees into the area. The letter to the German was the more specific one because the Nazi policies of the Germans had caused some of these problems. Italy merely served as a country from whose ports—and in whose ships—the refugees sailed for Shanghai.

The attitude of the Japanese authorities was most important because the Japanese occupied the area north of Soochow Creek, which was one of the few sections where accommodations could be found for the refugees. The Shanghai Municipal Council felt compelled to forbid the further entry of refugees into the International Settlement, but also stated that if the Japanese authorities relented in their own restrictive policies, the Council would cooperate in allowing Jews to enter. On August 17, 1939, the Council sent letters to all of the shipping companies in the area and asked them to avoid bookings of refugees who wished to come to Shanghai. In the letter, it was stated that: "It will be agreed that any temporary hardship which may be caused by refusing to accept bookings will be very much less than the hardship that would be caused if persons were allowed to book and leave for Shanghai."

With the outbreak of the war in Europe (on September 1, 1939), the flow of refugees from Central Europe, by way of ships, slowed down to a trickle. This made unnecessary the various measures taken by Shanghai officials prior to the war. The problem was now a new one: that of relatives joining those Jews who already had settled in Shanghai. The August regulation of the Council forbidding the further entry of refugees was now amended. It authorized entry of the following persons:

1. Those who had $400 in American money, if they were adults, and children who had $100 in United States currency or its equivalent in foreign money.

2. Those who had immediate relatives of refugees living in Shanghai, or those who were to marry Shanghai residents.

It is worth noting that the Shanghai Municipal Council regulations held for certain areas and not for others. For example, the section north of the Soochow Creek was subject to Japanese jurisdiction, even though this locality was technically part of the International Settlement.

In a letter to E. T. Nash, assistant secretary of the Council, the Japanese Consul, Ishiguro, promised to cooperate with the Council in regard to the refugee influx. The consul also dropped the demand that the refugees prove financial competence. This promise to drop harsh demands was reiterated in another epistle, this time from the Japanese Consul Miura, to Ellis Hayim of COMAR. This communication, dated, October 28, 1939, said, in part: "In consideration, however, of the desire of the refugee residents in the port of Shanghai to send for their relatives in Europe, the Japanese authorities may make, from a humanitarian standpoint, exceptions to the general rule, thereby permitting the entry thereinto of refugees in limited numbers."

On November 1, 1939, the vice chairman of COMAR, E. Kann, wrote to the Imperial Japanese Consul General and expressed the deep appreciation of COMAR for "Japan's humanitarian attitude in times of stress."

On this same day, November 1, the Jewish Problem Committee met in Tokyo to hear a report on recent developments on the Jewish situation. The speakers were Inuzuka and Yasue. Inuzuka's report was nothing special. In the main, he repeated his earlier statements. He said that the Jewish financial spokesmen and leaders were veering away from the British and that the Japanese contacts with Jewish leaders were proving to be useful to Japan because the Sassoons, the Kadoories and the

Abrahams were now turning toward Japan in friendship. He said that there was nothing to worry about concerning the Russian Jews, who were being held well in hand because of the success the Japanese were having with the Jews generally.

As an instance of Japanese success, Inuzuka spoke of the Pacific Trading Company, a brokerage firm controlled by Japanese, Chinese and Jews. A Mr. Ezekiel was reported to be one of the top officials of the company. He was a former chief accountant of Sir Victor Sassoon, and also his chief secretary.

Inuzuka also stressed the significance and importance of attempting to persuade the United States that Japan was treating Jews correctly. He offered these suggestions, among others: 1. that Japanese propaganda specialists guide Jewish leaders and rabbis; 2. that the Jewish spokesmen be persuaded to write articles favorable to Japan—and to pay them for the articles, if necessary; and 3. to place secret agents within Jewish groups so that the Japanese should know, at all times, what the Jews were doing.

Inuzuka reported that there were, at this time, some 8,800 refugees in Japanese-occupied territory and that 7,000 were receiving relief aid. Only ten had been affirmed as members of the Communist Party. He also pointed out that none of the many Jewish organizations were engaged in any subversive movements.

The German-Soviet Pact, he said, had disillusioned the Jews and therefore the influence of Soviet Russia had declined severely. He suggested the idea that the Jews had now been persuaded that they had no choice but to turn for support to the Japanese Armed Forces. He concluded his report by urging that propaganda and intelligence activities be intensified.

Colonel Yasue, in the second report offered at the meeting, began by remarking that the general Jewish situation in Manchuria was very good, which actually meant that the Japanese authorities were in full command of the situation and that the Jews were cooperating with them. He observed that when the

Jewish community of Dairen elected a president and officers, they turned to him, Colonel Yasue, and left the selection of the officers to him.

Nevertheless, Colonel Yasue was not entirely pleased by what was going on. He told the Jewish leaders something which disturbed everyone concerned. He reported that White Russians had informed the Japanese authorities that some Jews, mainly Soviet nationals, had sent a telegram to Sir Victor Sassoon, who was then in the United States—and to Jewish leaders in New York, Paris and London—that the Japanese navy was oppressive; that it had banned the entry of Jewish refugees to Japanese territory; that the navy had been putting pressure on Jewish businessmen; and that these Jews had called on Jews all over the world to rise up and fight against Japan.

Yasue was highly disturbed by this report. He demanded that the Jews investigate this matter and report to him. The Jewish community almost immediately denied the report and said it was entirely false. Colonel Yasue then suggested that the source of his information may have been Communist, and that the entire scheme was aimed at causing trouble between the Jews and Japan. But Sir Victor Sassoon had made an anti-Japanese declaration and the Shanghai Jewish Communal Association went on record to express its "deep gratitude towards the Japanese government for its just, humanitarian and unprejudiced attitude toward us."

Yasue also made mention of a plan—suggested to him by a group of Jews—to form an economic mission to visit countries in North and South America. It was also suggested to him that hundreds of rabbis, stranded in Japan, be moved to Shanghai.

The methods by which Japan was trying to get Jews on their side was also illuminated by Yasue's report. The colonel observed that it would be a good thing if the Jews arranged a secret meeting—with American Jewish representatives in attendance—to draft a petition, with the aid of the Japanese authorities, stressing the tolerance of Japan toward the Jews. The meeting, he said, should be made to appear as though it were voluntarily called by the Jews. And he said also that some Japanese nationals should be present at the meeting. He asked that this meeting be called for November of that year since the Jewish Conference would meet publicly in December. He concluded by stating that "My personal position toward the Jewish people is that I will do my best for them."

It should be remembered that both Inuzuka and Yasue did not always reflect the official thinking of the Japanese government or military services. All too frequently, their opinions were based on wishful thinking and on insufficient knowledge of the Jewish people.

The Japanese army and navy were not consistent in their view toward the Jews. At one time, these military branches were favorably disposed toward the Jews; then, again, they changed their minds. Japanese authorities in Tokyo, Shanghai and Manchuria were not especially friendly to the Jews, as is indicated in a message sent to the Japanese Ambassador in the United States, Horiuchi, by Minister Nomura. The message states, in part: "In view of the fact that negative opinion regarding advantageous employment of Jews was gaining ground, we were not necessarily enthusiastic about giving any positive consideration to this problem."

The Japanese, it is clear, had some doubts about the success of their negotiations with the Jews of Shanghai and of the United States. These doubts were clearly expressed by Inuzuka, when he attempted to challenge these doubts with arguments of his own. Inuzuka said that he had talked with a man named Murata, who had met with "Blandes" (who might have been Supreme Court Justice Louis D. Brandeis) and "other responsible and powerful Jews in America." Murata had been dealing with Jews for two decades and he was described by Inuzuka as a man who had faith in negotiating with the Jews. "The Jews," Inuzuka said, "should not be judged on the basis of telegrams. They are clever in bargaining—through the habits developed over two thousand years. If you were to change our positions by putting Japan in the difficult position of the Jews, you would understand that it is only natural to hide our weak points." He also explains the Jewish interest in helping German-Jewish refugees. "It is to be noted," he explained, "that the Jews in America— eighty per cent of them—are of German origin and have the same strong blood consciousness."

He added that Shanghai's Jews have not cooperated more fully "because they were not approached by responsible Japanese authorities." He supported Murata's suggestion that the Jews be cultivated. But Inuzuka, in another statement, revealed that he had another idea in mind as well: "To accommodate 30,000 Jews and have them under our influence in this national emergency is useful in another manner. It has a 'hostage' value, and in utilizing the financial power of these Jews has the effect of our holding a weapon over their heads." He made the further point that it was not difficult to find room for 30,000 Jews in China or Manchuria. In such vast areas, he said, 30,000 "are just like a drop of water in a large river." Thus, he urged that direct negotiations with Jewish representatives in America be continued. And he also urged that Japan utilize the technical skill of the refugees in rebuilding China.

In all their speculations, the Japanese took into account the powerful and influential Dr. Stephen S. Wise in the United States. They recognized in Dr. Wise a great Jewish leader on the American scene, and they continued to hope that a sympathetic Japanese policy toward the Jews would influence Dr. Wise and make him change his anti-Japanese views. His "influence over President Roosevelt's policy," they believed, would do much to alter the opinion of the United States government. Dr. Wise had written to a Dr. Karl Kinderman indicating the willingness of Jewish organizations to deal directly with Japanese officials.

Kinderman was a Jew who had taught school in Berlin. Unhappily, there is evidence that even though he was Jewish and anti-Soviet, Kinderman was in the employ of the Nazis. Dr. Wise rejected the idea of negotiating with Kinderman himself, but he did indicate that if the U.S. State Department approved, Jewish organizations would deal with the Japanese.

But in spite of these shafts of light in a dark picture, they remained only shafts of light. Nothing happened. The reality of the situation itself was overwhelming. World War II was in progress. There was a lack of shipping. There were other obstacles, too great for the average refugee to overcome.

The Japanese were upset that the Shanghai Municipal Council was being lenient in issuing permits to refugees. The Japanese Consul, Ishiguro, complained of this tolerance to E. T. Nash of the Council, and he wanted to know how many permits the Council had already issued to refugees who had $400 in American dollars. Ishiguro disclosed that the Japanese themselves had issued twenty-five certificates. Nash said that 555 had been issued by the Council and that the shipping companies had issued another seventy-seven. The Consul stated in his letter that there would be a tightening of controls. In a cable from Consul General Miura to Foreign Minister Arita, it was stated that all the refugees had now been registered and there were no other refugees in transit. The message admitted there was a possibility that there were unauthorized settlers in Japanese-occupied areas, but that a further check by naval officials would find them out.

The total number of applicants for registration was 10,418. Of this number, all but eighteen were registered, and these eighteen were being investigated. Some 2,000 of the refugees were without means and were living in a camp operated by COMAR; 134 were patients in COMAR-operated hospitals and the remaining 8,000 or so refugees were expected to live independently. Actually, the cable reveals, about 5,000 of the Jews were not independent, for they received $7.50 each a month, together with their meals at the camp. Thus, only 3,212 were on their own. Another 1,547 applications were on hand from members of families in Europe who hoped to join their relatives in Shanghai, but only forty-three certificates were issued to such persons.

This information presents in all its naked brutality, the sad facts of the situation at the time. And so all the talk of sympathy and humanitarianism means little in the face of these statistics. To bring the story forward even more clearly, here is the text of a telegram sent by Arita to Togo, the Japanese Ambassador in Russia: "In case Jews attempting to take refuge in Shanghai from the European war apply to your office—Moscow—for visa for Shanghai through Kwang-tung Leased Territory or Manchuria or via Tsuruga, it is advisable that no such visa be issued to them unless they have an entry certificate issued by the Imperial Consulate in Shanghai, even though they have that issued by the Shanghai Municipal Council or French Concession."

It should be pointed out that Tsuruga was the first point of debarkation near Kobe, Japan. This town played a key role as a transit station in 1940 and 1941. According to a report of the Jewish Relief Committee of Kobe, the total number of transients from this area were 2,493, as against 2,116 who arrived through Shimonoseki and Kobe directly. The total number of refugees aided by the Kobe Committe came to 4,608, of whom 2,178 arrived from Poland, 2,116 from Germany and 315 from other countries.

The information contained in the cable reflects the character of the refugee influx from ships via European ports to the Trans-Siberian Railroad, Manchuria and Japan. Of the 4,608 refugees who passed through Kobe between July, 1940 and August 1941, most were transients with visas to other countries. That is to say, the early refugees were truly transients. But from October, 1940 on, many were actually homeless, for they had left Poland—

following the invasion by Germany—into Lithuania. In Lithuania they organized themselves into special groups. One was called Bnei-Yeshiva, for they were rabbis and students of outstanding Lithuanian yeshivas, or rabbinical seminaries. Another was called chalutzim, or pioneers, and these people wanted to emigrate to Palestine.

Of these people, some 2,000 availed themselves of Japanese transit visas. They traveled, in extremely difficult winter conditions, on the Trans-Siberian Railroad, and they did not have any papers which would permit them to go elsewhere. Thanks to the tolerance of the Japanese, many of the transients (a transit visa was valid only for fourteen days), were permitted to remain on Japanese territory for two to eight months. During this time, they managed to arrange for proper visas. More than 1,000, however, failed to get new papers, and by November, 1941, they finally ended up in Shanghai.

CHAPTER III

THE NAZI REFUGEES

UP TO THIS POINT in our narrative, most of the information concerning the refugee has come from sources other than the refugees themselves. In the following pages, I shall attempt to collate and synthesize the personal accounts and eyewitness reports so that the refugees will speak for themselves and the reader will get an insight into the day-to-day problems of the refugees as they saw and experienced them.

It is a fascinating tale and it has been told in the past, in bits and pieces, by many reporters, individuals who have lived through the era, and by historians who have studied the era. Among the valuable papers from which material has been culled are these: M. Rosenfeld's three unfinished manuscripts on the history of the Jews of Shanghai, which were written in 1944 and are to be found in the YIVO archives in New York City; F. Reiss' "Report of the Medical Board, Committee for the Assistance of European Jewish Refugees in Shanghai," issued in Shanghai in April, 1940; Laura L. Margolis' "Race Against Time in Shanghai," an article published in *Survey Graphic* in 1944; the catalogue of the exhibition of "Jewish Life in Shanghai" sponsored by YIVO in 1950; D. Kranzler's dissertation on "The Shanghai Jewish Community," a 1958 paper written at Brooklyn College. There are, of course, others as well, but these will suffice for the present purpose of indicating the variety of studies.

I shall attempt to be factual and not dramatic, for the facts speak eloquently and are dramatic in themselves.

Because of Nazi repressions and persecutions, which commenced in 1938, between 17,000 and 19,000 Jews—who came from Central Europe—managed to reach ports in Italy and got on ships to Shanghai. Shanghai, it will be recalled, was comparatively easy to enter, for the officials there did not insist upon stringent formalities. In studying the statistics and figures offered by some of the writers listed above, it is clear that most of the refugees were middle-class Jews, people with homes and from the established professions, who were by no means eager to go to an area where the climate was poor and the economic situation difficult. The variety of occupational backgrounds, their comparatively advanced age and the wide range of nationalities made adjustment to a strange and alien land more complex. Moreover, while as many as ninety-two per cent were practicing or professed Jews, the others were either so-called "racial" Jews or Christians.

For example, on the matter of professions, Robert Barnett, in his study, "Economic Shanghai, Hostage to Politics," published in 1941, reports that there were 220 physicians; one hundred manual laborers; 120 cosmetic experts; 180 dentists; 120 nurses; 200 "agents," a rather vague category; 160 "household experts"; 220 hat makers; 130 engineers; 1,100 merchants; 260 musicians; one hundred female needle workers; 150 cooks; 140 butchers; 120 nurses for children and 100 chauffeurs. A Joint Distribution Committee (JDC) report on the religious breakdown reveals that of 15,000 refugees, 13,927 (or 92.9 per cent) were Jewish; 603 (or four per cent) were Protestants; 420 (or 2.6 per cent) were Catholics. There were eighty others.

The vast majority of the refugees arrived in Shanghai with little money, for Nazi Germany permitted the refugees to leave Germany or Europe with ten marks, or approximately $2.50 in

United States money. The question then arises as to how they were able to prove that they had the necessary $400 for entry. The Shanghai Municipal Council or the Japanese authorities allowed the men and women to land provided there was $400 held for them ashore. Usually, American friends or relatives sent the money, through American banks, to the Committee for Assistance. This money was held in a special account at the Chase Bank in Shanghai. Based on this money, the authorities issued "Landing Passes." These permits were presented to the steamship agency in Shanghai which, in turn, telegraphed their European offices to sell sailing tickets from Italy to Shanghai for the refugees who had money credited to them. Because of the war in the Pacific, tens of thousands of U.S. dollars remained in the Chase Bank because many refugees were unable to reach Shanghai.

The refugees carried with them their personal belongings and their professional and occupational skill; no more. Yet they also nurtured in their hearts great hopes for the future. They had, after all, escaped from the death furnaces of Europe and they expected to move on to more permanent places of settlement. This last thought should always be kept in mind, for none of the refugees expected to remain in Shanghai. It was, to them, merely a way station. Eventually, they hoped to move on, or to return to their homeland. They were, in mind, as well as in body, transients. This psychology of temporary settlement was of extreme importance both to the refugees themselves and to the resident Jews who, in spite of all the good will in the world, could not handle the thousands of incoming Jews in an organized and methodical manner.

The first problem, and one which never really was solved, was the matter of adequate housing. Until the war in the Pacific, there was housing to be found in three sectors of the city: in Japanese-occupied Hongkew, in the International Settlement and in the French Concession. There had been heavy fighting in

Hongkew in 1937, between the Chinese and the Japanese, and a goodly portion of the section had been destroyed. The housing that remained was poor and the inhabitants were mostly Chinese. The more desirable residential areas were in the International Settlement and in the French Concession, but there was not much room for newcomers in those areas. Thus, the bulk of the refugees were forced to move into Hongkew. As of January 19, 1940, the breakdown was as follows: 11,000 refugees in Hongkew; 1,500 in the International Settlement and 4,000 in the French Concession.

Two types of dwellings were made available in Hongkew: camps and what was known as Lane Housing. Lane Housing consisted of single-storey or two-storey houses situated on two sides of a narrow lane or alley leading off from the main thoroughfare. The houses were flimsily built, airless and dark. Each house had up to ten rooms, with primitive sanitary facilities which everyone had to share. The houses were owned by foreign or Chinese companies and were rented to the refugees. If a family had two rooms, it was considered to be well off, for most lived in one room and sublet a second room to other families, which were sometimes large. This arrangement had its good points. Apart from yielding some money, it gave the family renting the second room a sense of ownership.

These close living conditions were bad for normal living. Morals declined and there was much friction in families. Sometimes there were divorces and decent behavior was not as common as it would have been had these people been able to spread out and live more comfortably and spaciously. At the same time, this kind of existence sometimes led to mutual helpfulness. About 6,000 to 8,000 lived in these lane houses or one-room apartments.

Conditions were even worse in the camps, called by many "homes," taken from the German "heim." But these camps were far from homes; they were, in fact, camps. About 2,500 refugees lived in them. They were actually five old buildings which had survived bombardment. The entire area consisted of the ruins of five bombed-out edifices, rebuilt along the lines of a Chinese compound and was intended to accommodate 1,000 persons. The Ward Road Camp, which also housed the kitchen, was the headquarters for all the camps. There were two schools, an old Army barracks and a warehouse. The people slept in dormitories and each dormitory put up from twenty-eight to forty-two persons, although there are reports extant that there were as many as 150 in a dormitory. There were double-decker beds with a curtain for privacy—and the privacy was flimsy indeed. In the army barracks, for example, there were two antiquated toilets to serve 400 people. Because of the paucity of furniture or storage facilities, the refugees had to live out of their suitcases. Much of their belongings were destroyed by mildew caused by the humid climate.

There were three principal committees involved in caring for the refugees and their endless, constant needs. One was the International Committee (IC), which was also known as the Komor Committee (its first manager was Paul Komor). It was composed of wealthy Jews of Dutch and British citizenship. Among its members were Sir Victor Sassoon, Ellis Hayim, M. Speelman, R. D. Abrahams and others. A second group was made up of local residents. It called itself The Committee for the Assistance of European Jewish Refugees (COMAR). At first, it was headed by a Dr. Karl Marx, who left Shanghai in 1939. The third unit was the East Jew Committee, organized by the Ashkenazic Jewish community in May, 1941. Its chairman was Alfred Oppenheim and its vice chairman was Joseph Bitker. The aim of this committee was to take care of the refugees from Poland and Lithuania. All three committees got together to provide food, shelter and medical and financial assistance to the thousands of refugees coming into the area.

It must be remembered that Shanghai never had any organized social agencies as we understand them in the West. Up to this time, only the White Russians and the Portuguese carried on minor relief programs to take care of their own needy members. Destitute Chinese begged in the streets for alms or quietly froze to death in the cold winter.

The accomplishments of the various committees have been ranked as miraculous by contemporary impartial observers. In 1939 alone, more than 4,000,000 breakfasts, lunches and suppers were served free of charge or at a nominal cost to the occupants of the camps and private homes. Because the staff was not experienced and was a volunteer group, there was some difficulty in running the kitchen. There was poor management, and the kitchen help was untrained. The refugees waited in line a very long time for their food and after 1941 the already meager diet deteriorated. Thus, many of the refugees sold their personal belongings in order to supplement their rations.

Medical care was another immediate problem. Shanghai's general hospital facilities already were taxed to their utmost. Thus, new arrangements were required. A medical board was quickly organized and an emigrants hospital—with a seventy-five bed capacity—was put into operation. By 1940, it was expanded to a 200-bed hospital. In May, 1939, scarlet fever broke out and an isolation hospital had to be established. Major surgery and specialized cases were turned over to the municipal hospitals. The camps themselves had dispensaries, with doctors and nurses in attendance. There also was a pharmacy and eventually a maternity ward.

The precise cost of this relief program is difficult to determine, although it must have run into hundreds of thousands of dollars. While substantial sums of money were raised locally, the bulk of the money was contributed by the JDC to the IC (International Committee) in Shanghai, which legally represented COMAR in dealing with municipal, consular and overseas agencies. Rosenfeld, in his writings, accuses the various committees of being merely administrative bodies and that they exhibited no creative imagination in aiding the refugees. He writes of duplication, waste and red tape. Although there is, no doubt, much validity to his charges, it should be emphasized again that the confusion and inefficiency, where it existed, was due to the fact that the workers were volunteers and simply were not trained professionals in relief work.

It is, therefore, logical, that the JDC decided to send its own representative, Miss Laura L. Margolis, to survey the situation and to reorganize the International Committee. She arrived in May, 1941 and in November of the same year, Manuel Siegel came to help her. Unfortunately, they could not achieve very much, for the Pacific war broke out in December and the IC was automatically dissolved. The Japanese considered many of the IC members as enemy nationals and interned them.

As only 8,000 refugees were on limited relief, how did the remaining 10,000 manage to exist? In most instances, it was a matter of their adjusting to the harsh conditions or to utilizing, to the best of their abilities, their various skills and professions. Doctors, lawyers and engineers had it comparatively easy. They were permitted to go about their work without having to pass special examinations. All they had to do was to inform the authorities that they were there. This freedom and ease were to be found only in the International Settlements of Shanghai and Tientsin and other extraterritorial areas. It was far more difficult for professionals to operate in the territories occupied or controlled by the Japanese.

A number of the non-professionals managed to find jobs with export-import houses. With the war in Europe, there was a growing demand for goods manufactured in Shanghai and, in turn, brought increased business to the established Shanghai firms. Some refugees, thanks to the low currency exchange rate of the Shanghai dollar in relationship to the American dollar, managed to set up their own mail order businesses. Others established local firms and used their skills as leather and metal workers, designers, tailors, milliners, bakers and confectioners. They opened little shops and peddled their goods from door to door.

Meanwhile, in a period of less than three years, Hongkew was rebuilt. The rubble vanished and there arose these new shops as well as new houses with indoor plumbing and bathrooms. Chusan Road, once a small, dingy typical Chinese lane, now looked like a Vienna street, with sidewalk cafes, delicatessen shops and speciality shops as well. Even so, the goods produced by the refugees—usually of higher quality than the Chinese goods—were more expensive than the Chinese wares, and this made the competition fierce. It was difficult to survive economically, no matter how hard the refugees worked.

There were other limitations as well. For example, it was hard for Jews to move to other areas in China. Most of the immigrants had passports stamped with a "J" for Jew. Thus they were placed into a category of non-treaty subjects and consequently they required special permits from the Japanese authorities if they wanted to move to North China or Tientsin. Nevertheless, a handful managed and they did get to Tientsin, Harbin, Dairen, Tsingtao, which was a summer resort, and even to the mainland of Japan itself.

It was quite natural that so ambitious and individualistic a group of people should feel the need to organize their own religious, educational and cultural establishments. Most of the refugees who originated from Germany and Austria were accustomed to the Liberal or Reform type of service, with an organ and a mixed choir. This, of course, was alien to the Sephardic and Ashkenazic Jews in the region.

Up until November, 1941, the numerous Reform Jews held their High Holiday services in rented theatres. Then, in November, the "Juedische Gemeinde" dedicated its own synagogue on MacGregor Road. In the various camps themselves, the services were conservative.

The spiritual leaders themselves were organized into two

associations. One was called the Ihud Rabbanim; the other, Kolel Kovno-Vilna. They had a combined membership of eighty. The cantors, like the rabbis, also banded together and they had their own association of fifteen members. The establishment of the Gemeinde led to the formation of a Chevra Kadisha (Burial and Welfare Society) and a Ladies Auxiliary.

It is clear that the influx of these refugees gave a tremendous impetus to the religious life of the Sephardic and Ashkenazic communities. A new sense of friendship, responsibility and unity developed in the older settlers and they discovered that their own religious traditions, sometimes neglected, were being revived.

In addition to this trend and development, Rabbi Ashkenazi, the leader of the Russian Jewish community, found his own hand strengthened. He was now able to do more than ever before to raise the religious level of community activity. He and his friends started, for example, Hebrew schools, in two camps, for about 120 boys. The students were provided with free tuition, free food and clothing. In time, a Beth Jacob School for girls was established, with gratifying educational results.

Some of the refugee children attended the long-established Shanghai Jewish School for their non-religious training. Most of these children, however, were educated through the Shanghai Jewish Youth Association, which was organized and supported by Horace Kadoorie, an outstanding philanthropist. The Kadoorie family, one of the truly distinguished Jewish families in the Far East, were long associated with promoting education, for Jews and non-Jews alike.

The Shanghai Jewish Youth Association was opened in November, 1939 on Kinchow Road. In January, 1942 the school moved to more spacious and attractive quarters on East Yuhang Road. Even during the war, the school operated exceedingly efficiently and served some 700 students.

Another 150 students attended the Freysinger Jewish Elementary and Middle School, which was named after a refugee educator, Ismar Freysinger, and which started its operations in April, 1941. In addition to the 150 students, who attended daytime classes, there were 500 adults who took English courses in the evenings. In 1943, trade classes were added, sponsored by ORT, the Guild for Craftsmen, and by W. G. Tonn, an Oriental scholar.

All of these educational institutions did passably good jobs and played key roles in the community. There is no doubt that they were necessary and vital to the continuation of Jewish studies and survival.

It is, nevertheless, no exaggeration to state that the greatest spiritual and educational impact and influence were made by the Mirer Yeshiva. This group of deeply Orthodox and pious Jews, totalled only 300 persons, including entire families. They arrived in Shanghai in August, 1941. Mir, a little town in Lithuania, twenty miles from the Russian border, was a great seat of Jewish learning and the Mirer Yeshiva was one of the finest in the world. The group that reached Shanghai consisted of the entire faculty and student body of the yeshiva. The Hitler-Stalin Pact of 1939 threatened them with destruction and the group managed to escape, intact, first to Vilna and then to Kovno, major cities in Lithuania. Rabbi A. Kalmanowitz, the head of the yeshiva, worked tirelessly and effectively on behalf of the yeshiva and through his efforts, the unit escaped Europe and arrived in Kobe in February, 1941, following an arduous winter journey on the Trans-Siberian Railroad. Rabbi Kalmanowitz did much of his work from the United States. He persuaded the United States Department of State to convince the British representative in Lithuania to certify that every member of the yeshiva was a Polish citizen. It was in this fashion that the teachers and students received transit visas from the Japanese Consul in Kovno.

After the yeshiva contingent reached Kobe, they were unable to find refuge elsewhere. So they moved to Shanghai in August,

1941. Here they were met by a delegation of Jews headed by the venerable Rabbi Ashkenazi. This group made every effort to find shelter for the scholars and students. Above all, they sought for them a place to study. The Sephardic community turned over to them the spacious Beth Ahron synagogue, where they continued with their studies in the face of all difficulties. The synagogue, situated at 50 Museum Road, was built in 1927 by S. A. Hardoon, a wealthy Sephardic Jew. This synagogue had rarely been used by the Sephardic community, which utilized another synagogue for its religious activities.

In order for the yeshiva students to continue their studies, a number of problems had to be resolved. To begin with, they lacked the holy books which they needed for their studies. But the entire *Shas*, a complete set of the Talmud, plus many specialized rabbinic volumes were reprinted through the process of photo-offset, thanks to the generosity of local Jews. Not only did the yeshiva students continue with their work; some of their leading scholars produced new rabbinical tomes.

While the Mirer Yeshiva was the largest group of its kind, there were other yeshiva groups from Kamenets, Kletsk, Lubavitch, Lublin, Telsh and others.

These students, scholars and teachers introduced into Shanghai an aura of piety and a sense of courage at a time when these qualities and virtues were most needed.

Other refugees who tried their utmost to work at their professions were writers, musicians and artists. Some of the musicians found jobs in the local orchestra and in amusement areas and elsewhere where there was some entertainment. The vast majority of the artists, however, performed and produced for their own refugee groups. There were many plays staged and quite naturally the experience of the refugees themselves frequently were the themes played on the stage.

There also were extensive sports activities. The Jews organized their own soccer league and built an excellent field on what had been a deserted piece of land. The first soccer match took place on April 23, 1939 between teams of the Jewish Recreation Club and the Ward Road Camp.

The refugees, who showed great resourcefulness throughout the difficult years in the Far East, were particularly imaginative in their attempts to survive as a people in the period just before war broke out in the Pacific.

As Japan and the United States were not yet in conflict, the sea routes to the free world—and especially to the United States—were still open and the flow of relief funds and ease of communications were most helpful.

Thus, within a short period of no more than three years, the Jews, in fact, created a new settlement which took on all of the aspects of a busy small town. When the two JDC workers from the United States arrived in 1941, hope grew high that the relief and emigration program would become more systematic and more effectively organized.

When Japan attacked Pearl Harbor and actively joined the Axis nations of Germany and Italy, the hopes of the Jews were all but crushed. Almost immediately, many British and American firms were closed down, which meant that many refugees lost their jobs or were unable to continue their own small business enterprises. In addition, the war in the Pacific meant that relief funds from overseas would be halted. Moreover, the JDC representatives, who were American citizens, expected to be interned at once. While they were not interned until more than a year later, the constant uncertainty of their position and the fear that they might be picked up any day at any time, cut into the day-by-day effectiveness of the relief program.

Fortunately, Miss Margolis had become friendly with Captain Inuzuka, whose understanding attitude made possible the release of some frozen currency and of 5,000 bags of cracked wheat supplied by the American Red Cross. Captain Inuzuka stipulated that the two JDC workers now take over the entire administration of refugee relief activities. This was done. The JDC representatives helped to create a new committee recruited from Shanghai residents acceptable to the Japanese. The previous committee (the IC) had been dissolved with the outbreak of the war because its members were enemy aliens.

The Japanese laid down three conditions under which the committee could continue to operate:

a. No loans for the relief program could be obtained from "enemy nationals."
b. No donations could be obtained from "enemy nationals."
c. No funds could be obtained from enemy countries abroad.

This, of course, made it very difficult for the JDC to work effectively, for as early as 1942 even those Jews who were financially able to lend money to the JDC were afraid to do so. Appeals through the press did produce some money. The publicity, however, irritated the Japanese, who issued orders—which were never carried out—for the arrest of Miss Margolis and Mr. Siegel. The money which was lent to the JDC, incidentally, was repaid after the war.

In order to avoid a complete breakdown in the relief program, the JDC had to cut its food rations to the refugees. As a result, only 4,000 of the 8,000 persons on relief, received their daily bowl of stew. In the face of great difficulties, kitchen operations were organized so that they were more effective than ever before, even though the staff was reduced to a bare minimum.

The shortage of funds forced the closing down of two refugee hospitals in July, 1942. This was a most unhappy period because it was the hottest time of the year and it has been recorded that sixteen persons died in a single July day from the heat. Nevertheless things did not come to a standstill. A kitchen-fund committee was begun in August, 1942 under the sponsorship of the JDC in cooperation with those Jewish organizations still permitted to exist. They were the HIAS (Hebrew Immigrant Aid

Society) and the Kehilla, both of which were labeled as non-political by the Japanese. While the kitchen fund committee expected originally only to help in obtaining food for the poorest of the refugees, it soon found itself saddled with additional tasks, such as the reopening of the hospital, the operating of a kindergarten and an orphanage. But no matter how much work was done the situation deteriorated rapidly, particularly in the camps. Here the lack of soap, the inability to obtain clean and fresh underwear, the extremely crowded conditions—all of these factors made it impossible for the people to maintain cleanliness. One result was that the camp was soon infested with lice.

In a desperate attempt to avoid contamination, the relief officials issued to the camp residents overalls made out of cotton flour bags. This "uniform" made the refugee feel like an outcast.

It is no wonder that a few dozen resorted to begging, morale slipped. There was a sharp increase in crime, in divorces. Even prostitution flourished and it was necessary to register prostitutes. According to available records seven Jewish women were registered prostitutes. But some women formed illicit relations with unaffiliated men in order to obtain more food and better living conditions. In a few instances, this was done with the full knowledge of their husbands who shared in whatever material advantages there were.

As an illustration of the sad situation, twenty mothers sold their newly-born children to the highest bidder. Here is another significant story which must be recorded which reveals the situation of the children. Obviously, the lack of recreational facilities and the cramped family quarters were particularly depressing for the young boys and girls. Thus, the story is told when a mother told her six year old son—who had been born in the Shanghai camp—that a three-room apartment awaited them in a new home and a new country, the boy said, "Mommie, we must be sure to get the place near the window and no upper bed."

CHAPTER IV

JAPANESE POLICY ON
THE REFUGEES

THE MOMENT the Japanese bombed Pearl Harbor and brought the United States into the war, the Japanese policy towards foreigners living in Shanghai changed radically. Beginning with December, 1941 the Japanese considered all these people enemy nationals. There were about 10,000 such foreigners in Shanghai, which was now occupied by Japan. They included 8,000 British subjects, some 2,000 Americans and a handful of Dutch subjects as well as others.

While they all expected to be interned almost immediately, it took the Japanese more than a full year of preparing and planning before they issued orders for internment. They preferred to call it "segregation."

Thus foreigners were able to maintain their positions in industry and government throughout the entire year of 1942; under Japanese supervision of course. In this manner, the Japanese were able to take over existing establishments in a smooth fashion, in a way which did not harm their war effort.

There were also significant changes in the treatment of the Jewish refugees. Up to the time of Pearl Harbor, it was Japanese policy to treat the Jews decently so as to persuade foreign investors to establish business in the Far East and to avert the aggravation of relations with England and the United States.

Now, with the Japanese fighting on the side of Germany and Italy, it was no longer necessary for the Japanese to consider the reactions and attitudes of other powers. The result was that the Japanese arrived at a new policy which featured three main points.

1. The admission of Jews into Japan, Manchuria, China and other Japanese-occupied territory was to be prohibited, except for special cases.

2. As a general rule, Jews already residing in the above listed areas, were to be accorded the rights due them on the basis of the citizen papers they held, but in view of their "racial characteristics" they, their homes and their business were to be closely watched and hostile activities were to be eliminated. By hostile activities was meant anti-Japanese actions. Notice also the phraseology now took on the spirit of Nazism as the Japanese talked of racial characteristics.

3. Jews who could be used by Japan were to be well-treated, but no support would be given to the Jewish national movement, meaning Zionism.

These three points indicate some of the dilemmas in which the Japanese policy makers found themselves. Curiously enough, these dilemmas ultimately made them responsible for the survival of the refugees and the resident Jews. On the one hand, the Japanese were aware of the extermination policy of the Nazis and they were impressed by Germany's impressive military victories. The Nazi persecution of Jews had driven nearly 20,000 people to Shanghai, presenting the Japanese with a situation they had never before faced. On the other hand, the Japanese knew that if they were to emulate the Germans, these acts would be used as counter-propaganda by England and the United States. Under these conditions the Japanese clarified their position. They stated that as a general rule, Jewish people who

formerly held German nationality would be considered stateless
and would be accorded the same treatment as the White Russians. Telegrams to this effect had been sent in January, 1942
from the Foreign Ministry of Japan to the ambassadors in Manchuria and China and to the Consulates General in Shanghai
and Peking. The Japanese explanation stated "it is deemed
appropriate that only so much surveillance as is necessary be
exercised over them."

It is natural that as the Japanese thought in terms of "surveillance," that they eventually began to think in the direction
of establishment of a special area for Jews. There is documentary
evidence that the navy established such a plan, which was
approved by the central government. While the navy had been
responsible for the plan, it did not wish to be the sole enforcing
agency. Instead, the Ministry of Greater East Asia was to be
responsible for the enforcement, with cooperation from the army
and the navy. The plan had two objectives:

1. To set up a Jewish district in the Hongkew area and
    to bring twenty thousand refugees into the area.
2. To dispose of the White Russians and other Jews later
    on.

Both objectives are quite revealing; they indicate who the
navy planners believed were the undesirable and dangerous elements in the country. Obviously, the Nazis already had some
influence on this new Japanese policy toward the Jews. Much
of the Nazi influence must have taken effect in the months
between the Liaison Conference 1942 and the navy plan of
November the same year. The plans of the conference were
mild and flexible, compared to the strict measures proclaimed
by the navy a few months later.

Nazi pressure grew stronger during September, 1942 with
the arrival in Shanghai of three high-ranking Nazis in that year.
They were Robert Meisinger, known as the "Executioner of War-

saw"; Adolph Puttkammer and Hans Neumann, both of whom had experimented on Jews in Auschwitz and Bergen-Belsen.

While the exact nature of their mission was not clearly known, it is obvious that they advised their Japanese allies on how to deal with the Jews. This has been confirmed by the former German Consul General of Tientsin, Fritz Wiedemann and Lieut. Col. Takashima a former Japanese intelligence officer at Shanghai.

The German's statement, made on January 22, 1951, asserted that: "I hereby declare that I was thoroughly acquainted with the situation in the part of China then occupied by Japan, and that I followed the directives of the German government in all my activities there."

Fritz Wiedemann's statement continues: "I therefore confirm that the internment of Central European emigrants and as a rule primarily Jews who had emigrated from Germany and Austria to China had taken place upon the instigation of the German government then in power. The Japanese themselves were not anti-Semitic, and we were under orders to instruct the Japanese authorities about the racial policies of Germany and to suggest appropriate measures. There was no doubt in my mind that the internment of the Jews in the Shanghai ghetto had been instigated by German authorities. From my work with Hitler I know that in the matter of policy, pressure was exerted upon friendly governments in that direction."

Lieut. Col. Takashima came from a prominent Japanese family and in 1935 graduated from Tokyo University as a specialist in German literature. He continued his German studies at Berlin University while he was stationed in Berlin. After Pearl Harbor, he was sent to Shanghai as an Intelligence officer. From April, 1942 to October of the same year he was stationed in Saigon, but returned to Shanghai in October and remained there for nearly a year. In private discussions with him, Takashima said that the Shanghai ghetto was established under Nazi pressure and there was no truth to the rumors that the Japanese built a concentration camp in the city. The arrival of these three Nazis in Shanghai caused a flurry of rumors about new plans to exterminate the Jews, rumors which added to the anxiety of the refugees. This fear and worry lasted until the end of the war in 1945.

While extermination plans never materialized—most fortunately—measures to limit the movement of the refugees and to keep them in a segregated area were soon put into effect. In August, 1942 a Vice Consul at the Shanghai Consulate, Mr. Shibota, notified the leaders of the Jewish community—unofficially and confidentially—that the Japanese were under heavy pressure from the German Consul to isolate the Jews, particularly the refugees. The Germans, Shibota stated, stressed the fact that most of the refugees were Jews and were, therefore, enemies of Hitler and devoutly desired the defeat of both Japan and Germany; thus, he emphasized, the Germans asserted that the Jews had to be carefully watched for possible acts of sabotage. They urged the isolation of the Jews.

One of the areas of isolation suggested was an island at the mouth of the Yangtze River near Shanghai. The Hongkew district was another area mentioned. Shibota, who apparently was anti-Nazi himself, implied that in his opinion the Jewish community might well organize itself and to call upon all its available sources to help soften the severity of the conditions which might be imposed in the near future.

We can obtain a better idea of the mood of the Jews from an eye-witness account from Mr. Bitker, who reported: "We left the meeting in great alarm as we pondered the as yet unknown fate which imminently confronted the Jewish community. At this time the Germans were still victorious and Stalingrad was surrounded. The Japanese, too, were having their share of victories, and it appeared that only a miracle could change the tide. We decided to continue to confer among ourselves, but to avoid the creation of a feeling of panic in Shanghai in order not to disclose that we had been tipped off by Shibota. However, information like this has a tendency to spread like wildfire and within twenty-four hours the entire community knew what had transpired.

"As a result, information about the meeting in Mr. Speelman's residence leaked out to the Japanese authorities, particularly the Foreign Division of the Japanese Gendarmerie, then quartered in the infamous Bridge House, where the Japanese held prisoners charged with espionage, sabotage and other hostile acts against the Japanese. The Japanese arrested all of us who had attended the meeting, and we were all locked up separately in order to make communication among ourselves impossible.

"I was brought in for questioning after three or four days, and it was made very clear to me that they knew all about the meeting, about Shibota, and what was discussed. I was asked to state what I knew about the meeting and when I attempted to gloss over some details in order not to embarrass Shibota, I was prompted in such a manner as to make it eminently clear that they had all the facts. Subsequently we were all released—some sooner than others. It is interesting to note that they assured me that the possibilities that had stirred up the commotion were not realistic because the Japanese authorities were always fair and just to everyone. When I pointed out that the source of our information was an officer of their own Japanese Consulate, I was told that he also would be arrested and brought in for questioning. You can imagine my amazement when a few days later I saw Mr. Shibota, in his underwear, in a nearby cell, a prisoner like the rest of us. . . . We later learned that Mr. Shibota was cashiered from his post in the consular service and sent back to Japan, never to be heard from again. The fact remains, however, that as a result of the leak of information to our community before the Japanese were ready to make an official announcement, the restrictions planned for refugees were not implemented until February, 1943."

Early in the month of February, preparations had been sufficiently advanced for the army and navy commanders to formulate an official proclamation which was eventually issued on February 18 of that year.

The proclamation contained these four paragraphs:

1. Because of military necessity, the residential and business areas of stateless refugees in the Shanghai area will be restricted to an area within the International Settlement east of the line connecting Chohoro, Mokairo and Todotsudo, west of Yoyuho Creek, north of the line connecting Toshikobairo, Mokairo and Kaisanro, and south of the boundary of the International Settlement.

2. Stateless refugees presently residing and/or operating businesses outside the area mentioned in the preceding paragraph shall move their residence and/or places of business inside the above prescribed area by (month, day) from the date of this proclamation. Those desiring to buy or sell or rent houses, stores and other installations located outside the above area which are homes and/or business places of stateless refugees shall obtain prior approval of the authorities concerned.

3. Those other than stateless refugees may not move into the area designated in paragraph 1 without permission.

4. Any person who violates this proclamation and interferes with its enforcement shall be punished.

The key word of the proclamation was "stateless"—for this meant all the refugees from Germany, including Nazi-occupied Austria and Czechoslovakia, Hungary, Poland, Latvia, Lithuania and Estonia, who had arrived in Shanghai after 1937. The Jewish residents of Russian origin and all the White Russians were specifically excluded from this proclamation since it was assumed that "there was no particular danger of their causing international complications." This statement is ambiguous, for it could mean that the non-internment of the White Russians and the Russian Jews would not affect Japan's relations with Germany. It could also mean that Japan's relations with Russia, then still neutral, would not be affected by this policy.

Actually, neither White Russians nor the Russian Jews were Soviet citizens, which fact could have made them stateless in the eyes of the Japanese. However, since they were potentially Soviet citizens, the Japanese were reluctant to intern them at this time.

On the day of the proclamation, the newspapers carried detailed instructions concerning wives (the non-stateless wife was to be treated like her stateless husband) or business partners (who were to be treated as stateless) even though they themselves were not stateless, but were married to or connected with stateless persons. These instructions also covered possible extensions of the removal date and transfer of property outside the designated area. A warning was issued that unreasonable profits were not to be made out of the sale of properties belonging to persons who had to move into the designated area. Finally, it was announced that a special office for Shanghai Stateless Refugee Affairs had been created, which would be headed by a Mr. T. Kubota, a man whose decisions were to affect the lives of every Jew in Shanghai for the next two-and-a-half years.

One does not require a great deal of imagination to appreciate the impact of this proclamation on the lives of the refugees. After four years of hard labor and untiring efforts to establish themselves in the midst of alien surroundings, more than 8,000 men, women and children were ordered to rid themselves of their homes, earned with difficulty, their shops and their offices and to move into a small, overcrowded area jammed with refugees. They now had to yield up the personal freedom they had enjoyed in Shanghai. From this point forward, the Jews were unable to do anything without the permission of Kubota. It was on his orders that there was organized the Shanghai Ashkenazi Collaborating Relief Association (better known as SACRA).

The minutes of the SACRA meetings, though carefully edited, provide us with a vivid picture of the daily problems that arose on the matter of the transfer of the Jews from one section to another. The minutes also offer an insight into the work of SACRA and its position within the community.

Ten days after the proclamation was issued, a committee of eighteen met to deal with the problems raised by this edict. The chairman of SACRA, and its leading personality, was Dr. J. A. Cohn, of a Turkish-Jewish family. Dr. Cohn had received his medical education in Japan and his background and contacts with the Japanese made him a welcome person among the Japanese, especially since he spoke Japanese fluently.

The official proceedings of SACRA attempted to give the impression that the organization was initiated by the members of the Shanghai Ashkenazi community. But it is now known that the members met—most reluctantly—and on the orders of the Japanese. Joseph Bitker, who was quoted earlier in this narrative, was a key member of SACRA, although he was not an officer of the Ashkenazic community. Nevertheless, his post as treasurer and financial advisor of the committee made him an important personage. He was not distrusted as Dr. Cohn was, for the SACRA members were not entirely sure of Dr. Cohn's motives. Bitker said this about the entire set-up:

"Kubota emphatically advised the established residents not affected by the proclamation to form their own committee to aid the refugees on the matter of resettlement. . . . Our community very reluctantly submitted to the suggestion of the authorities, but in confidential deliberations among ourselves, we decided to assist the refugees but to delay as long as possible their removal from the International Settlement and French Concession, using every form of sabotage that was possible. . . . The work of this new committee was thankless, unpopular and misunderstood by many refugees, as it was not feasible to explain to thousands what we were trying to do. We hoped that by stalling the implementation of the rehabilitation as long as possible, we might hope for a turn in the fortunes of war."

The honorary advisor to the main committee of SACRA was M. Kano, a Japanese friend of Dr. Cohn. The very fact that he held a position in SACRA was another reason for the refugees to dislike and distrust SACRA. The committee itself was subdivided into subcommittees on Finance, Housing, Application (which handled applications for extensions of removal dates), Economics, the Press and Law. Other working subcommittees were to be organized from among the German and Polish refugees on the same matters, and these subcommittees were to be governed by a Joint Administrative Committee (JAC), which was to report to the main committee of SACRA.

This involved organizational apparatus ran into immediate trouble with the Polish refugees, who objected to be classified as "stateless." They refused to participate in the workings of the group and to name their own representatives to the committee. They addressed a letter to Dr. Cohn, asking him to intervene with the Japanese on their behalf. They pointed out that their chances for emigration depended upon their retaining their status as Polish citizens, represented by a Polish government. Their request, they hastened to add, in no way affected their deep feelings of appreciation to the Japanese nation which had offered them the shelter that others had refused them.

The opposition of the Poles, although not successful, was well organized, and the fact that they were unwilling to participate with the other refugees irritated the Japanese. There were only 1,000 such Poles, but their attitude was bothersome.

Among the Polish Jews were many who had fought against the Nazis in organized political groups. Some of them were thrown into the Bridge House for their opposition and contracted typhus. According to one prisoner, O. Lewin, life in the prison was extremely harsh. "We had to live in cells with thirty-five persons," he wrote, "where we were forced to sit in a squatting position all day long without being permitted to lean against the wall, or to stretch our limbs or to talk. . . . A hole in a corner served as a toilet, and it was cleaned out only once a day, thus spreading a terrifying stench in the cell. Despite severe cold, we were forced to undress completely every day to cleanse our clothing of lice. The lice alone made life almost unbearable. Without exception, every prisoner found sixty to seventy lice on his body each day." The writer of this report himself contracted typhus.

It is worth noting that half of the Polish refugees were members of various rabbinical academies and that the representative for the housing committee was a rabbi.

Kubota himself attended the second meeting of SACRA in order to expedite the work of the unit. He told the representatives that the Japanese authorities had no interest in the property of the refugees and they had no reason to become upset or panicky. Although it may have been true that the Japanese were not pressing the Jews on their property (merely taking advantage of the situation where Jews were forced to sell at a loss), the statement indicates the mood of the refugees following the issuance of the proclamation. It was easy to understand the mood of depression. The refugees saw, before their eyes, their homes diminish in value; they realized how hard it would be to obtain new housing in the area into which they had to go.

One of SACRA's first problems was how to raise the money for its operations. At first, it was thought that SH$1,500,000 would be needed. (At the 1942 rate of exchange, SH$ 20 was worth one American dollar; which makes the sum $75,000.) The committee actually believed it would have no difficulty in obtaining this sum. At the same time, the leaders of the group were realistic enough to know that, if necessary, they would ask Kano or Kubota to sign letters making the contributions obligatory. It was also decided to register all refugees through SACRA and to caution the "Juedische Gemeinde" not to issue any instructions without SACRA authorization.

The biggest problem, of course, was housing. Early in March

there were some plans afoot to renovate a Chinese school and a Salvation Army building. There also were some plans to take over forty-eight houses occupied by Chinese and to negotiate for an additional 200 houses owned by members of the Ashkenazi community but occupied, without contracts, by Chinese. To finance these and other long-range housing projects, SACRA was to ask Kubota to arrange for credit for fifteen to twenty years for the sum of five million Yen. The United States dollar equivalent is not known, but it must have been a considerable sum for Mr. Kano, the honorary advisor to SACRA, received 1,000 Yen a month.

To make sure that the plans of SACRA received maximum publicity, the organization's leaders invited the editor of the local paper, *Our Life,* to attend all meetings, but nothing was to be published without the prior approval of the Presidium.

By the end of March, it was already obvious that the shopkeepers would not be able to find adequate space for their businesses by May 18. Through the Joint Administrative Committee, a letter was addressed to SACRA asking for an extension on the deadline. This request was taken up by Dr. Cohn personally with Kubota, who gave an extension of three to six months for businesses only. The owners of the businesses would have to abide by the May 18 deadline and find housing for themselves. There was a hitch here, too. In applying for the extension, the shopkeepers had to indicate "how much they would be willing to contribute voluntarily to the funds of SACRA."

Most of the refugees were members of the "Juedische Gemeinde," which, in turn, was governed by a duly-elected board of officers. But the Japanese were not satisfied with the way they operated their own community, so they dismissed the elected officers and placed more "suitable" persons into their positions, men who were totally unqualified to be communal leaders. A SACRA member was to be their supervisor. This act gives some idea to the historian that the German Jews, as well as the Polish Jews, tried to resist the pressure of the Japanese and to slow down the enforcement of the restrictive measures.

But even with the best of intentions, the average refugee encountered so much red tape that his removal would be delayed even after he found a new home in the designated area. By early April, the Polish representatives were informed that their request for exempt status had been denied and that they, too, would have to move.

Because of the congestion in the area and the oncoming summer heat, the danger of epidemic grew. SACRA, therefore, made plans to give vaccines to all the refugees and to establish a small isolation hospital.

Other projects were also planned. One was aimed to familiarize the Japanese with Jewish literature. While this was an interesting idea, we do not know how it worked out. SACRA issued bulletins, which appeared in supplements of the local Jewish newspaper *Unser Leben*.

By April 28, only two buildings were placed at the disposal of SACRA, the Chinese school and the Salvation Army building, but the renovation was not completed in time for the Jews who had to move in. There was still some hope that the forty-eight houses on Ward Road would be obtained, but they, too, needed rebuilding. Thus, the committee would be able to provide shelter for about 1,000 persons. Some 2,000 had found places on their own. This meant that 5,000 were without roofs over their heads.

A special meeting was called in order to apprise Kubota of the situation. But Kubota did not depend upon SACRA for information. He replied to them, in turn, that according to the police reports which were available to him, there would be homes for 4,000 Jews by May 18. Another 2,700, he declared, would be allotted housing in various buildings and if these places were not ready in time, these people would receive extensions. Further extensions were given to doctors, medical personnel and other specialized cases, but these amounted to no more than 500 persons.

Kubota made it appear that the housing problem was not insuperable. Nevertheless, the three-month waiting period was tense and nerve-wracking. There was so much tension in the air, as a matter of fact, that Kubota found it necessary to write an article for the *Shanghai Jewish Chronicle* (which appeared on May 9, nine days before the deadline.) In it, Kubota paid tribute to the refugees for abiding by the proclamation and ascribed the rapid results to SACRA's assistance and the "sacrificial" attitude taken by those Japanese residents within the designated area who voluntarily offered their homes for the use of the refugees. He overstated the case somewhat since the Japanese were given the opportunity to move from a less desirable location to a better one. In his article, Kubota reported that there still were a number of persons who were—unnecessarily—afraid to move into the designated area and that there also were unscrupulous persons who had asked for exorbitant sums of money from the refugees for houses in the sector to which they were obliged to move. He warned that the authorities would not countenance any interference with the execution of the proclamation. All applications for extensions, he wrote, had been carefully screened and, in some cases, had been granted. The refugees were urged to report all those who had charged them unfair prices for shelter, for without such information the authorities would not be able to act. This entire subject was academic because the refugee was grateful when he found a place to live or a customer to buy his shop. The authorities, on the other hand, were fully aware of the profiteering but closed their eyes to it by placing the burden of proof on the harassed refugee. Kubota also observed that "the area designated in the proclamation is neither a ghetto nor a jail, but an area which is full of hope for the refugees in which they may build a haven for themselves where they may carry on peacefully with great advantage to themselves."

At this point, we may well examine the question as to whether or not the area was a ghetto. The dictionary definition of a ghetto is the quarter of the city in which Jews are restricted. By this definition, Hongkew surely was a ghetto. The measures taken by the Japanese to restrict the refugees to a particular area led the Jews to call the designated area a ghetto, for no one was allowed to leave the sector without a special pass, which had to be renewed constantly.

The Japanese official who was most responsible for the internal operation of the ghetto itself was a Mr. Ghoya. He has been considered, by people who dealt with him, a psychopathic personality. He called himself "King of the Jews," and loved to be photographed in front of a line of people waiting for passes. He displayed all the characteristics of a tyrant. He wanted to be feared and, at the same time, to be loved and to be popular. He would play with the children and then tyrannize their parents. He had almost complete control of the passes, which were stamped with a "J" for Jew, and carried a yellow stripe across the top. In order to leave the ghetto, the refugees needed, in addition to a pass, a red badge which had on it the words, in Chinese, "May pass." Later on, those refugee Jews outside the ghetto had to wear a Star of David.

The ghetto area itself was closed off by barbed wire and rope. In order to check on passes and other regulations, the Japanese utilized the Vigilance Corps, known as Foreign Pao Chia. "Pao" means unit in Chinese. The corps had been organized by the Shanghai Municipal Council to assist in routine police duties. When the ghetto was established it was given the task of policing all foreigners entering and leaving the ghetto. It was a particularly unpleasant task because it was made up of 3,500 male refugees, from the ages of twenty to forty-five. They were divided into forty-five units and under the supervision of the

Japanese chief of the Wayside Police Station. These refugees themselves were constantly checked in the performance of their duties by the regular police. The officers of the Vigilance Corps were particularly hated by the residents, who felt that the corps collaborated too eagerly and efficiently with their Japanese masters.

It was common knowledge for example, that those who broke the rules were often turned over to a Mr. Okura, a Japanese, whose duty it was to punish those who broke regulations. Thus, many Jews were beaten severely and imprisoned in the typhus-infested bunker.

The period from the spring of 1943 until the summer of 1944 is without doubt the most critical period spent by refugees in Shanghai. Because of their transfer to the ghetto, most of them had no money and relief sums from the JDC had stopped coming in, while local contributions were not enough to cover the increasing needs of the refugees. Some financial support was given by the Jewish community of Tientsin. There was also some hope that money would be forthcoming from Harbin. In September, 1943, 100,000 Swiss francs were placed at the disposal of the Red Cross for the Aid Society of the Polish Refugees on condition that SACRA would exercise no control over the money. The fact that SACRA did not insist on control is eloquent evidence of the shortage of funds which led the SACRA authorities to accept these conditions and to appreciate any money that came from the outside, even though the distribution of this money challenged SACRA's own position.

The SACRA's minutes of June and July speak openly of the urgent need for local funds and the sorry plight of the refugees. From an official Japanese report—prepared by Takeji Takahasi, a police inspector of the Ministry of Greater East Asia and the Chief of Police of the Yojuho Police Station—we learn that the situation was an extreme one. This police report observes that stricter control was needed of the refugees, who, though registered as ghetto inhabitants, continued to live on the outside. The report mentions that the daily bread ration for the 2,783 residents and the 2,105 newcomers was nine ounces. In addition, there were 3,500 persons, including 500 children, who received one meal a day. Thus, more than half of the refugee population was on very small relief rations. The report stresses the rising prices, the diminishing relief funds and the strenuous efforts on the part of the refugees to obtain money on which to live. An immediate result was the increase in the number of street peddlers, of whom there were now about 170, and the number was constantly rising.

While the shortage of goods was due to the war—a situation beyond the scope and solution of the refugee organizations—the shortage of money was a problem with which they did try to deal. SACRA planned another assessment and a special collection for relief, but they ran into difficulties because the same people had already been hit twice for assessments. SACRA thought of other projects to bring in money, including a lottery, according to the Japanese police report.

This report also states that there were 400 families which had set up stalls to sell their own winter clothing in order to obtain food. SACRA planned a bakery to make sure that there would be enough bread for the refugees. They were encouraged by the fact that the Japanese had authorized the use of 10,000 pounds of flour a day. It is not known how any of these plans worked out, but it is known that in July, 1943 there was 7,000 unemployed refugees in the ghetto and their chances of finding employment diminished as time went on.

It is no wonder that the physical and moral strength of the refugees deteriorated rapidly. They were forced to live on about 1,300 calories a day, which was enough to keep them from starvation, but not enough to keep them in good health. The mortality rate was high and more than half of the 400 patients treated in the dispensaries lost from twenty-five to seventy pounds.

RABBI MEIR ASHKENAZI
Spiritual Leader of Russian (Ashkenazic) Jewish Community of Shanghai
from 1925-1947
Died in New York City 1956

Entrance to the Jewish Community Center, Shibuya, Tokyo, Japan, June, 1957

PROFESSOR MASAYUKI KOBAYASHI
Japanese scholar and authority on Jewish history.
Collaborated on part of the book.

COLONEL SENKO YASUE
Important figure in Japanese Jewish relations prior to and during World War II

First Far Eastern Conference, Harbin, 1937
Conference addressed by Manchurian Official
Jewish Honor Guard in background: also Japanese and Jewish flags side by side

Mirer Yeshiva Students arriving in Kobe, Japan, 1940

Passover Seder in Tokyo, 1957

Headtable l. to r.:

Partially hidden: U.S. Consul General Lindsay, his wife, Captain Leon Kintberger, USN, Mrs. H. Dicker, Chaplain Dicker, Mrs. Kintberger, Prince Mikasa, Joseph I. Linton, Israeli Minister to Japan.

Scene: Jewish Religious School Children ask the 4 questions.

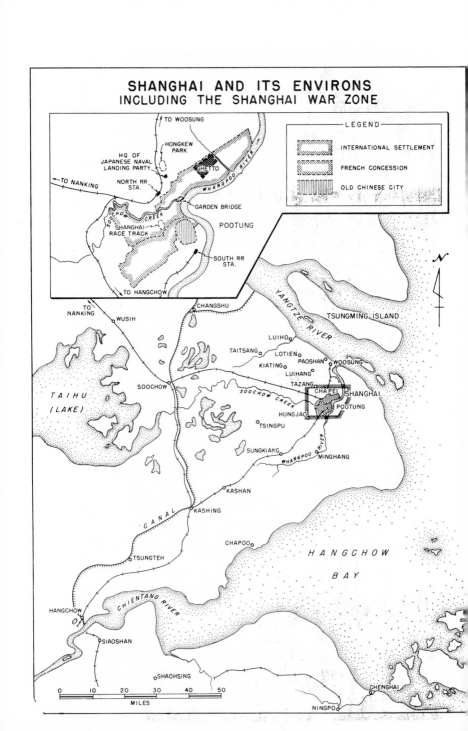

SHANGHAI AND ITS ENVIRONS
INCLUDING THE SHANGHAI WAR ZONE

LEGEND

INTERNATIONAL SETTLEMENT

FRENCH CONCESSION

OLD CHINESE CITY

TO WOOSUNG

HONGKEW PARK

HQ OF JAPANESE NAVAL LANDING PARTY

GHETTO

TO NANKING

NORTH RR STA.

GARDEN BRIDGE

WHANGPOO RIVER

POOTUNG

SOOCHOW CREEK

SHANGHAI RACE TRACK

SOUTH RR STA.

TO HANGCHOW

N

TO NANKING

CHANGSHU

WUSIH

YANGTZE RIVER

TSUNGMING ISLAND

LUIHO

TAITSANG

LOTIEN

PAOSHAN

WOOSUNG

KIATING

LUIHANG

TAZANG

SOOCHOW

SOOCHOW CREEK

CHAPEI

SHANGHAI

POOTUNG

TAIHU (LAKE)

HUNGJAO

TSINGPU

SUNGKIANG

WHANGPOO RIVER

MINGHANG

KASHAN

CANAL

KASHING

CHAPOO

HANGCHOW BAY

TSUNGTEH

CHIENTANG RIVER

HANGCHOW

SIAOSHAN

SHAOHSING

CHENGHAI

NINGPO

0   10   20   30   40   50

MILES

In the face of this situation, the Japanese nevertheless attempted to draw from this group manpower for labor and military chores. They planned to utilize the Jews and divided them into four categories:

1. Those who were of vigorous health and were capable of any kind of work.
2. Those who may not have been vigorous but were nevertheless able to work because of their special skills or intelligence.
3. Those who were not strong but were capable of some work.
4. Those who were unable to perform any kind of work.

It may appear from the foregoing that in 1943 the Japanese authorities were interested only in moving the refugees into a ghetto and exploiting them. But this is not the case. There was a special report prepared by a Mr. Murakawa, a Vice Consul in the Shanghai Consulate General on the Russian Jewish community of Shanghai. This report was sent to the Minister of Foreign Affairs. It is a lengthy report and deals with the communal activities of the Russian Jewish community and their leaders. The report includes an analysis of three organizations of approximately 5,000 Ashkenazi Jews, hitherto unmentioned. These units are a Consumers Association, a Chamber of Commerce and a Russo-Jewish People Society. These groups, together with the other organized Russian Jews, grew in importance in the history of this era because these Jews were the only ones in Shanghai to enjoy some freedom.

There are some anti-Jewish observations in the report concerning the objectives and political affiliations of the Russian Jews. Some 2,000 of them were registered with the Russian Refugee Committee, while over 3,000 had passports from Soviet Russia, Poland, Portugal or China. The main spirit of the report is indicated by these quotations from it: "However, no matter what kind of passports they may have or no matter what camps they may belong to, they all work for the Soviet Union. . . .

The Jews in Russia were masters of the Soviet people up to the time of the German-Soviet war, and they still are masters at the present time. . . . The Jewish religion under the Soviet Union has become a National religion. . . . No matter what circumstances Jews may be in, they all work for the advantage of the Soviet Union. . . ."

There is recurring evidence that the Japanese viewed with great suspicion the activities of the members of the Ashkenazic community, some of whom were protected by their Soviet passports and some by their status as "receipt citizens." "Receipt citizenship" could be acquired by any Russian Jew by writing to the Soviet Consul and applying for Soviet citizenship. Even though the applicant may have had no intention to follow through on his application, the receipt he was given offered him protection from the Japanese. It is a good guess that neither the Soviet passport nor the "receipt citizenship" would have done the Jews any good had the Axis beaten the Allies.

1944

With the beginning of 1944, there was no marked change in the situation relating to the refugees, but there were some minor signs—which we recognize more clearly in retrospect—that there was a slight improvement of their lot.

Now that nearly all the refugees had been relocated, the future operations of SACRA became a matter of debate among its committee members and its supporters. It is evident that the members themselves did not support the Japanese measures which SACRA had to carry out. Early in the life of the organization, there were some plans promulgated to reorganize SACRA on a commercial basis. But as time passed there were fewer and fewer meetings and some talk of closing down SACRA altogether. This lack of enthusiasm to continue the organization makes clear that the Ashkenazic community and the refugees did not support SACRA as an organization. It is not that they objected to the assessment of money, but to SACRA's interference in communal affairs. The lines of responsibility between SACRA and the Communal Association had begun to fade. Moreover, there were so many committees and subcommittees that in the end no one knew who was doing what, with whom, or where.

Not only were the Ashkenazi Jews suspicious of the Japanese and SACRA, but even the refugees distrusted them. It became apparent that Dr. Cohn and Kubota now had to decide whether or not to allow SACRA to continue its existence. Both of them felt that to close her down after only one year of operations would destroy the work it had done in the past. Nevertheless, there was agreement that reorganization of SACRA was in order.

The main feature of the reorganization called for the participation of men who would be more active in the community. These persons were to form a new committee, with Kubota serving as honorary chairman.

While on the surface this may seem to have been a rebuff for Dr. Cohn, who had been the honorary chairman, it really meant that SACRA would be given new teeth and Dr. Cohn would receive stronger backing. Under this new plan, each department would be headed by skilled staff members. All donations to SACRA would come from taxes and those who would avoid paying taxes would be reported to the office of the Shanghai Stateless Refugee Affairs (which meant Kubota) for compulsory payment. Finally, SACRA would now concern itself only with refugee matters and with issues involving the ghetto area. The Shanghai Ashkenazic Community Association would once again be in charge of the Jewish hospital, the school, the shelterhouse, the synagogue, the cemetery. The Association would also handle the funds for these institutions.

All of these plans led to the formation of a new committee

called the Central Control Board, with Dr. Cohn as Chairman. This board was to supervise all the organizations dealing with problems of the Jews in the designated area. It was a small body made up of SACRA, the JDC, the Kitchen Fund, the "Juedische Gemeinde" and the Permanent Investigation Committee (PIC). SACRA continued to function, in a diminishing fashion, until June, 1945, when its functions were absorbed by the Kitchen Fund. The Permanent Investigation Committee had been formed in November, 1944 at Dr. Cohn's suggestion, and served as a watchdog committee.

The Kitchen Fund had developed into the most important relief agency in the area since its establishment in 1942. At that time it had served lunches for about 1,500 persons. Its relief program now covered more than 10,000 persons. Its expansion had been made possible through funds it was receiving, through indirect channels, from the JDC, whose contribution covered about ninety per cent of the total relief budget.

An interesting human sideline to the collection of funds can now be told. Prior to her repatriation in September, 1943 Miss Margolis of JDC was a patient in a local hospital. She was frequently visited by Mr. Bitker, at personal risk to himself. These two people discussed strategy in the hospital on how to get funds from the United States, with the approval of the State Department, and send it to Shanghai through Swiss, Portuguese and Swedish committees. The approval of the State Department was to be communicated to Mr. Bitker in the form of a birthday telegram to his daughter. This telegram finally arrived early in 1944, at a time when the plight of the Shanghai refugees was desperate.

Thus, when the funds arrived, needy persons were supplied not only with food but also with cash. This was particularly important during the summer months, when only 5,500 hot meals could be prepared at one time through the Kitchen Fund facilities.

From the little information that is available, it is evident that the operation of the Kitchen Fund was difficult and full of problems. The trouble led to the formation of the Permanent Investigation Committee, which was to consist of two members of the Kitchen Fund and two more of the "Juedische Gemeinde," whose members were the principal beneficiaries of the Kitchen Fund. Other members included one representative each of the Chamber of Commerce, the Emigrants Residents Union and the Pao Chia.

The function of the PIC was to take on the operations of the Kitchen Fund or any other relief organization. From now on, all applications for relief had to be approved by PIC, after they had been processed by the individual relief organizations.

It is not difficult to understand that the vast relief activities required strict supervision. Frequently, the very people who were connected with the purchase and distribution of supplies and cash, were the same people—together with their relatives and friends—who were dependent upon relief. Undoubtedly there was some favoritism and minor irregularities here and there. But it is to the credit of the total relief operation that no reports have come down of Jewish officials taking undue advantage of their position.

The disadvantage of having so many committees was that needy people had to wait such a long time before they received what they required. For example, a refugee may have needed socks and shoes. After his application was investigated, by the "Juedische Gemeinde," he would get the socks immediately. The shoes, however, were considered a major item and their issuance had to be approved by the PIC. The PIC, in turn, would take at least two weeks to decide on the matter. It is no wonder, then, that there were many complaints. It was also believed by many that a person on relief received more than a person who worked for a living.

Generally, however, there was a definite upturn in the morale of the refugees, who closely followed the war in Europe. As the Allies advanced and the German Armies retreated on all fronts, it is natural that the refugees felt better about their own situation. The Japanese were fully aware of this development. As a matter of fact, the impending defeat of the Nazi regime strengthened the hands of those within Japanese circles who wanted to come to terms with the Allies. On the local scene, this meant that there was a softening attitude toward the refugees. This development led to the dismissal of Ghoya and a more generous pass system. But there was still a good deal of danger faced by the refugees. The increased strength of the Allies and their bombing attacks on China placed the refugees in Hongkew in peril, for the Japanese had stored ammunition and oil in the segregated district, which now was a prime military target.

On July 17, 1945, just before the war ended, a bombing attack on a Japanese radio station was followed by a direct hit on a refugee camp, killing 30 residents and wounding many more. A number of houses within the camp collapsed. Nevertheless there was no panic. Emergency dispensaries were quickly established and when the handful of available bandages were used up, the refugees turned in their linens and shirts to take care of the Chinese and casualties who were being treated in the same dispensaries. This act was deeply appreciated by the Chinese, who brought food, cakes and money to demonstrate their gratitude to the Jews.

There was, however, real excitement on the night of August 10, 1945 when the news of Japan's surrender spread like wildfire throughout the camps, Hongkew and all of Shanghai. The ghetto signs were quickly torn down and once again there was freedom in the air.

CHAPTER V

RED CHINA AND THE
JEWISH COMMUNITY

IN RETROSPECT, one must recognize one of the major developments in the history of Jewish life in China. This came about when the Japanese left in August, 1945, and when the Chinese Communist Armies moved into the Shanghai area in November, 1948.

The departure of the Japanese was of utmost significance to the refugees; the coming of the Red Armies was of overwhelming importance to the resident Jews. But the narrative may flow more smoothly and clearly if we deal with each unit separately, even though there was considerable interrelationship and interdependence between groups and events.

For the refugees, the departure of the Japanese was a boon. Living conditions improved gradually and the outlook for the future brightened considerably. Gone were the trivial and harassing regulations which had made life miserable and nearly unbearable. There was a new freedom of movement, which allowed some of the refugees to resume their former occupations and to move back into their old quarters in Hongkew. Nevertheless, it was not easy for them to regain their economic independence. Thus, for months after the liberation, most of the

15,000 refugees continued to depend upon outside assistance, which concerned their living quarters and their ultimate emigration.

The responsibility for both was assumed by the United Nations Relief and Rehabilitation Organization (UNRRA) and the JDC. In evaluating the work of UNRRA on behalf of the Jewish refugees in Shanghai, one must constantly keep in mind the over-all tasks of this organization in China.

These tasks were so tremendous that they stagger the imagination. It has been estimated, for example, that some 260,000,000 Chinese had been living under Japanese domination and that when the war ended, the Chinese government and UNRRA were faced with the urgent problem of providing relief for these Chinese—without adequate facilities or funds.

While the UNRRA allocation of $535,000,000 in American money was the largest sum given for the relief of any of the liberated countries, the sum came to no more than $2.00 for each individual Chinese. Nevertheless, UNRRA's aid to the comparatively small number of Jewish refugees was of vital value. The fact that the refugees were in the port city of Shanghai enabled them to obtain the maximum benefit from the first shipments of food and local surplus army supplies.

The JDC worked in conjunction with UNRRA whenever and wherever help was needed. Two new JDC workers, Charles Jordan and his deputy, Aaron Grodsky, came to Shanghai to direct the operation. They understood that the renovation of the camps and lane houses had to be fixed—as the first order of business, for they knew that many of the refugees would not be able to leave their houses for quite a while. As of the early months of 1947, for instance, there still were 3,000 refugees living under those difficult conditions.

Leaky roofs were repaired, recreational facilities were added, the area was cleaned up and the number of occupants to each dormitory was reduced. Additional sleeping quarters were provided through the use of UNRRA's Quonset huts. These huts were also utilized to increase hospital beds to a total of 186, which cut the waiting time for the admission of patients.

Generally speaking, the improvement in medical services was enormous. Another morale builder was the contribution of an ambulance by the American soldiers stationed in Okinawa. This project had been initiated by a Jewish soldier stationed there. Twice a month, more than 5,000 persons received relief from the JDC, which also distributed UNRRA's supplies of food and clothing to more than 9,000 refugees. Infant care was improved through enlarged maternity wards and a nursery. The JDC established a community center with a library and a reading room for young people. This center quickly developed into a social center and the focal point for cultural activities as well.

To carry out its ambitious, widespread and imaginative program, the JDC employed more than 200 refugees. The U.S. Army also hired refugees, many of whom were skilled workers. By March, 1946, nearly 1,500 men had been put to work by the U.S. Army. But there was more than just a job at stake here. The refugees saw in the Americans the symbol of the victorious future and as a result of their work with them, felt a great deal better than they had for many years.

When they met and talked with many American Jewish soldiers, they realized that the men in the uniform of the American Army understood their tragic situation and had deep sympathy for them.

In October, 1945, the Jewish chaplains Alvin I. Fine and Morris Gordon organized musical programs and "get-acquainted" parties. This program was started by the National Jewish Welfare Board, the agency through which the American Jewish community channeled its generous support for the men of the American Armed forces.

Only an American rabbi in uniform could have spoken to the refugees eloquently and understandingly, on the occasion of Passover. Chaplain Leon M. Adler arrived in Shanghai in 1946, two weeks before the first Passover after the liberation. Passover is the ancient festival celebrating the freedom of the Egyptian slaves from bondage. The chaplain said that his heart was full because of what he had seen and he told his audience that on the basis of his experience in Shanghai he was now beginning to understand what had happened to Jewry everywhere. He told the refugees that he and they were members of the same people; that their suffering was his suffering and that their misery was his misery. They took special comfort in his words, when he said: "I have heard the stories of the respectable, educated, honest Jews in Germany, Austria, Poland, Czechoslovakia and elsewhere. They were Jews as secure and at home in their society as we American Jews consider ourselves at home in ours, and see how they live! I can visualize the contrast between their former positions and their present ones, for now I can at least see one end of the tragic chain of their wanderings from Europe across Asia to Shanghai. I have heard of the miseries of the Hongkew ghetto where no money was coming in from outside sources. I have heard the stories of families or individuals in Shanghai who remain alone in this world, bereft of their nearest and dearest at the hands of the Nazi beasts. My emotions, my heart, are being added to my mind, my head, in the deep sympathy I feel for you. I have no right to commend you for the courage and endurance many of you have displayed, for commendation entails judgment, but I can admire it. Admiration, however, is cheaply given.

"More is needed and more is deserved. And so I promise you that I shall do all in my power to try to repay you for what you have suffered though innocent for the wrongs that had been committed against you."

It was words like these which brought new hope to 15,000 men and women who had to start life anew, to a group of people half of whom were between thirty-one and fifty years of age, and one-third were fifty years old or more. It gave them the desire to participate in cultural and social activities which had been almost forgotten during the years of the Japanese occupation.

Emigration

Soon after the end of hostilities, it became apparent that no matter how much their general situation would improve, the refugees had no real way of solving their many problems. Emigration was the only real solution. Since most of them had come to the Far East as transients, it was only logical that they did not wish to remain where they had been forced to live against their own will.

Of course, this raised the question as to where they could go. By this time, most of them had discovered that the rumors they had heard of the extermination of six million Jews by the Nazis were a bitter reality. Therefore, for most of them—especially those who came from Germany—repatriation to their countries of birth was inconceivable.

Ultimately the two countries which absorbed most of the Jews from China were Israel and United States. Those who left in 1946 and 1947 went, in the main, to the United States. Those who emigrated in 1948 and 1949 went, in the great majority, to Israel.

In addition to UNRRA and the JDC, the HIAS also carried on a tremendous program of assistance for the refugees. This agency, with its history of three decades of continuous work in the Far East, received communications and financial support for the refugees from relatives living abroad. HIAS also helped the refugees to obtain immigration permits and put them in touch with other survivors of the war years through the exchange of lists of names. In 1946, 157 persons received entry permits for Brazil, Colombia, Argentina, Peru, Venezuela, Uruguay, France and South Africa. There were 584 permits received for Australia and 1,795 affidavits for the United States.

The Resident Jews

While the Central European refugees saw very early that emigration was the only solution to their problem, the situation was different for the members of the Sephardic and Ashkenazi Jewish communities. They or their families had lived in Shanghai for two or three generations. Their communities totalled some 5,000, with the Sephardim representing about ten to fifteen per cent of this number. The Sephardim had suffered more heavily at the hands of the Japanese because they had been interned as enemy nationals during the war years.

Little is known of the functioning of the religious institutions during this period except for the Shanghai Jewish School, which up to 1941, had been operated by the Sephardim. Later, the management of the School was taken over by the Educational Aid Society, which was controlled by the Ashkenazim. In 1945, a Joint School Board was formed, but it is significant to learn that its chairman was not a Sephardi, which indicates that the Ashkenazi community had come of age and had moved into positions of communal responsibility.

It is evident from two particular actions that the Ashkenazim intended to remain in Shanghai and in China. In Shanghai they had sold the premises which had served as a club during the war years for more than $200,000, and had purchased a large plot of land in the heart of the French Concession. They invested more than $500,000 for new and luxurious facilities. The second factor which indicates that the Ashkenazim planned to remain in China, involved the problem of passports. Most of these Jews, Russian by birth and language, did not carry Soviet passports. Thus, in the eyes of the Chinese they were considered Stateless, and according to the current Chinese decree, the lack of a Soviet passport would have made impossible their further stay in China. So these Stateless, Russian-born Jews found themselves in a difficult situation. They wanted to remain, but they were reluctant to accept the outstretched hand of the Soviet authorities who offered them complete forgiveness and passports which would have afforded them status in the eyes of the Chinese.

The Jews knew they could not place much faith in Soviet promises of protection. They consulted with United States Intelligence officials who informed them that if they wanted to remain in China, they would have to take Soviet citizenship. It was as if these people had a premonition that Russian passports would create severe obstacles for them if they later tried to gain admission to the United States.

This passport obstacle later proved fatal to many would-be immigrants to the United States when they fled the Communists in 1948. This situation provides a clear picture of the actual homelessness and lack of status of the Ashkenazi community. They had first come to Shanghai when they fled the revolution in 1917 and, later, the Japanese invasion of Manchuria in 1931. They had tried to rebuild their lives in the strange cities of China—Shanghai, Tientsin, Mukden and Dairen. It is, therefore, not difficult to understand why they constantly felt a strong tie to the Zionist movement, especially the militant Revisionists. Most of the Jewish youngsters belonged to B'rith Trumpeldor and Betar. For these youngsters who had grown up in the remote corners of China, it was important that they parade in the uniform of the Revisionist youth groups. It meant more than merely having fun or participating in a parade. It generated within the hearts of these homeless youths a sense of belonging and gave them a sense of status in an international society.

The Zionistic feelings of these Jews increased in 1946 and 1947 when the Jews of Palestine and the Zionist movement throughout the world struggled to establish a state in Palestine following debate in the United Nations on the Palestine problem. There was a tremendous outpouring of sympathy and money during the battle for an independent Jewish state, after the United Nations partition decision.

On May 1, 1947, for example, a mass meeting was held in Hongkew, where more than 8,000 Jews protested against the hanging of Dov Gruner by the British authorities in Palestine. Attempts were also made to secure the act of support of Sun Fo son of Dr. Sun Yat-sen and a prominent member of the Chinese Nationalist Government, who was asked to endorse his father's sympathetic views on behalf of the Zionist movement. While the Jewish community provided generous support for the efforts to establish a state in Palestine, many of the old-timers did not expect to leave for Israel themselves. Thus, there was little preparation or schooling for a new life in Israel. Many of them hoped to remain in Shanghai where they worked so hard and successfully. While it would have been fairly easy to dispose of their properties and businesses prior to the arrival of the Communists, most of them were caught unprepared and had to leave many of their belongings behind.

On the eve of the big Communist offensive in 1948, frantic efforts were made to evacuate all the residents of Shanghai who were most likely to suffer at the hands of the new regime. The American government was deeply involved in these rescue operations, under the leadership of John Moore Cabot, the able United States Consul General in Shanghai. The State Department in Washington, via the United States Embassy in Nanking, continually sent him urgent messages to help the Shanghai residents in peril. On November 17, 1948, William H. Tuck, Director General of the International Refugee Organization (IRO), received a cable directed to him in Geneva from Charles E. Saltzman, Assistant Secretary of State for Occupied Areas. In this cable, the State Department urged the IRO "to evacuate 5,000 Jews, 8,000 White Russians and forty Polish refugees all concentrated in the Shanghai area." The Department had been advised that the State of Israel had offered asylum to the Jewish refugees. The question was whether IRO could provide the necessary ships to transport them to Israel. As for the White Russian and Polish refugees, there was no permanent haven in sight for them at the time.

Everybody concerned looked to Japan and General Douglas MacArthur in the hope that arrangements might be made for the temporary evacuation of the refugees to Japan. But General MacArthur, the Allied Commander, said that "Japan was not feasible as a base for the refugees." He made the statement in answer to an appeal by the German and Russian Emigrant Association, which represented 8,000 White Russians.

On November 18, Tuck replied to Saltzman that IRO's two ships, *Wooster Victory* and *Castelbianca,* with a total capacity of 1,772 passengers, could shuttle Jews from China to Japan to Australia, from which point they could be shipped to Palestine. Interestingly, in the cable the word "Palestine" was used instead of "Israel." Meanwhile, the IRO was cabling Australia for transit facilities. However, the use of these ships would be made possible only if the IRO were authorized to use three of their U.S. Army Transport Ships (USATS) on the Australian run in order to avoid disrupting transportation to and from Australia. Further, authority was requested for the USATS vessels to put into Palestine ports and to bring back to Australia Jews who had formerly lived in China. Only USATS ships were assured passage through the Suez Canal. In his cable, Tuck urged that General MacArthur again be asked to provide a temporary refuge in Japan for the refugees. A survey of Taiwan (Formosa) had shown that this island had no facilities for a temporary haven, for there was scarcely enough room in Taiwan to house the officials of the Chinese Government and the diplomatic corps.

On November 20, the State Department urged the Under-

Secretary of the Army to grant permission for the use of USATS ships outside of the Atlantic Ocean waters to make the run to Australia. Since it would not be feasible to put into Israel ports, temporary debarkation in Italy would be preferable. The plan was for Jewish organizations to transfer the refugees from Italy to Israel. In a cable dated November 23, Saltzman suggested to Tuck that Genoa be used as a port for the movement of refugees to Israel. He also suggested that the *Wooster Victory* and the *Castelbianca* proceed immediately to Shanghai to take on 1,700 refugees.

Saltzman also inquired whether Australia had granted the transit facilities and, if they had not, he wanted to know whether IRO ships on the Australian run could pick up refugees from Shanghai on their return voyage for delivery to their Mediterranean ports. By November 30, 1948, Under-Secretary of the Army Paul Draper had concurred with Saltzman's request for the use of three ships—which were on loan to the IRO—for one round trip from Europe to Australia to facilitate the evacuation of Jewish refugees from Shanghai. On the matter of the 8,000 White Russians, General MacArthur suggested that they be transferred to the Philippines or to the Southern complex of China.

That there were intensive efforts made to escape the Communists is indicated further in a cable by Cabot to the State Department on December 20, 1948. This cable is based on a report which held that "some questionable White Russians" found it easier to be evacuated under the IRO Displaced Persons program rather than as bona-fide White Russians. There were then 2,000 such Russians in Shanghai, all of whom had taken out Soviet passports, giving them up and applying for Stateless passports from the Chinese government. They then applied for membership in the White Russian Emigrant Association, which carefully screened them to make sure that they had an anti-Soviet background. Those who were rejected on the ground that they were not sufficiently anti-Soviet, found it easier to get out of Shanghai under the IRO program than did the persons who were in good standing with the White Russian Emigrant Association. The report also states that the Soviet Consulate encouraged Soviet passport holders not to repudiate publicly their Soviet citizenship when they turned in their passports. The Soviet Consulate continued holding their passports for further use. Later, these people applied for Stateless passports, which enabled the Soviet government to smuggle them in as spies into foreign countries. Thus, the report concludes, many Russians "keep a leg on each side."

I have no way of ascertaining whether the report in Cabot's cable presents an accurate picture. In this report, no names, facts or evidence are given. What does emerge is a spirit of intrigue and accusation which must have existed at that time in these emigrant circles. These people were drowning and they were trying to grab at anything that would help them safely to shore. Some of them felt that their own chances of escaping would improve if they accused others of pro-Soviet leanings. All too frequently in their lives these people had been engulfed by hatred and persecution and had barely managed to survive. In these hectic days, no one had the time or the patience to sift carefully the personal histories of all the applicants. This, of course, made it extremely difficult for the authorities to make satisfactory decisions in cases where some of the evidence was based on hearsay or on anonymous accusations.

It is apparent also in these accusations that the White Russians felt that the Russian and other Jewish refugees were not quite as homeless as the White Russians were. There may well have been a touch of jealousy in the charges as well, for the emergence of Israel made it possible for nearly 4,000 Jews to leave Shanghai for the new state within the short period between December, 1948 and April, 1949.

The influx of refugees into Israel began when Cabot urged

the State Department (in a cable dated December 21) to remove 2,500 refugees, who already had been screened, to an area under American control. Cabot pointed out that this act would strengthen the moral position of the United States when the American government would ask other nations to receive refugees. At the same time, George Hoague, Jr., the IRO's shipping expert, called on Mr. Sebald, the acting U.S. Political advisor for Japan and on General MacArthur to ask them to find a haven for 800 refugees. These refugees had held Soviet passports, which they had renounced, and were in danger of being liquidated during the Communist take-over. Moreover, Hoague wanted to discuss with them once again a plan to house in Japan 13,000 additional refugees. The end result of his visit was that he obtained approval to fly 150 D.P.'s to Japan for a sixty-day stay under IRO care. A second result of the meeting was that General MacArthur sent a telegram to a Philippine official asking that the Philippine Republic accommodate 8,000 refugees.

The hope that Australia might furnish transit facilities for Jewish refugees soon faded. In a talk between the State Department official and the member of the Australian Embassy in Washington, the Australian advanced four reasons as to why his government would not furnish the facilities. One, Australia had promised to absorb 100,000 D.P.'s within the next eighteen months and this effort would strain the country's existing facilities. Two, Australia already had admitted 15,000 Jewish D.P.'s since the end of the war and felt that it had done more than its share. Three, since the White Russians of Shanghai were not involved, Australia would be embarrassed by singling out only one group—the Jews—for favored treatment. Four, the Jewish community of Australia would use whatever pressure it could to keep some of the Jewish D.P.'s in Australia permanently.

The State Department official countered with the suggestion that Australia agree to accept no more than 2,500 Jewish D.P.'s in transit at any one time in order to utilize fully the ships which were returning without passengers from Australia to Europe. The Australian official gave no immediate reaction to this suggestion.

Faced with this negative outlook, the State Department approached the French government (on January 11, 1949) and asked it to make place for Jews in Madagascar and New Caledonia. In reply, the French said they might be prepared to talk about it, but this was no time for lengthy discussions.

By January, 1949, it became clear that most of the White Russians would be resettled, for the Philippine government had offered 6,000 of them a temporary haven for four months. On March 16, 1949 Cabot cabled the State Department that 5,000 had been transferred to the island of Samar in the Philippines. A month later, Cabot was able to report to Washington that only 1,300 White Russians remained in Shanghai and that the IRO contemplated no further transfers. Thus, the curtain was closed on the mass evacuation of this particular group of refugees.

The diplomatic correspondence with the State Department reveals some of the problems connected with the evacuation of the Jews. The American President Lines, for example, had asked the State Department for permission to ship 4,500 refugees to Israel on the *General Gordon*. This operation was sponsored jointly by the IRO and JDC. There was to be immediate trans-shipment of the refugees from the port of arrival on the West Coast to New York. The refugees were then to be moved to an IRO ship which was to go to Genoa or Naples. The U.S. Immigration Department had approved this shipment subject to two conditions. First, the persons involved had to have clearance by the American Consul of Shanghai. Second, men of military age, from eighteen to forty-five were to be excluded from this shipment. Fortunately, the second condition was cancelled five days later, since "there were so many heads of families among them."

This situation provides a sharp insight into the tensions prevailing at that time. We can only guess about the anxieties that prevailed in the five-day period when the condition was set on men of military age and then cancelled. No doubt, they were five days of living hell for the individual families who were faced with the danger of being separated. They must have been five days of frantic intervention on the part of some officials to force a change in the stringent rulings of the Immigration Department.

Another cable disclosed another problem. There were 2,600 Europeans—probably all of them Jewish—who refused to be evacuated because they had their hopes set on entering the United States, as they had applied for American visas as long ago as 1938.

These Europeans, according to the cable, were not interested in settling in Israel, since all their family ties and their interests were in the United States. It would seem unfortunate, it was stated in the cable, if the group with the strongest pro-American feelings should be left behind the Iron Curtain.

At this late date it cannot be ascertained how many of these people managed to reach the United States and how many of them eventually settled in Israel or elsewhere. It must be emphasized that the problem of immigration was not the exclusive responsibility of the IRO, the JDC, the Jewish Agency and various consulates. Many of the refugees, perhaps thousands, made their own private arrangements. Therefore, when the Communists eventually took over Shanghai, they found the city with practically no Jews and most of the Jewish property left behind.

Fortunately, the Communists allowed Tientsin's 800 Jews to leave the city. At first, it was feared that these Jews would be detained. However, the authorities were generous and allowed the Jewish emigrants to leave with most of their personal belongings.

In the beginning, Harbin's 1,800 Jews did not plan to leave en masse. Most of the local Jews were Soviet passport holders. They refrained from applying for exit visas because the local Soviet Consul issued an official announcement declaring that

Jewish citizens of Soviet Russia should not think of emigrating to any other country. Thus, they waited until a more lenient Chinese Communist policy enabled them to leave for Israel.

There is an interesting footnote to the story of the exodus from China. There was the question of the magnificent Jewish Clubs of Tientsin and Shanghai. The Jewish Club of Shanghai represented an investment of more than $500,000. In October, 1948 Boris Solomonik, the acting president of the Club, was called in to the Soviet Consul, and was urged to follow the example of the Jews of Tientsin, and transfer the Jewish Club to the Association of Soviet Citizens, to which some of the Club members belonged. Solomonik was fully aware such action was not in line with the wishes of those who had built the club. He stalled the Russians, and delayed giving them a definite answer, and, finally, in February, 1949, he recommended that the club be given to the State of Israel. His decision was approved and the key to this magnificent structure was formally presented to Moshe Yuval, Israel's consular representative in the city.

The rest of the dramatic and sad story of the exodus of the Jews from China is carefully detailed in the reports of the Council of the Jewish Community of Shanghai. This Council was organized on June 1, 1949 and was a continuation of the Far Eastern Emergency Council. It assumed the painful but necessary task of making the exodus as orderly as possible, and, at the same time, to assure the continuation of those activities which were necessary to keep the remaining Jews alive.

By August, 1950, the JDC closed its offices in Shanghai and the Far Eastern office of the Jewish Agency for Palestine moved to Hong Kong where it continued its rescue operations. The closing of these offices made the Council the only local agency through which relief and emigration aid were channeled. Its chairman until August, 1956, was R. D. Abraham, whose family had been for generations active on behalf of the Jews in China.

In 1949 and 1950 thousands of Jews left China. In the following years, only hundreds managed to get out and it was becoming increasingly difficult to find a place for those refugees who were old and sick.

These people, handicapped by illness and age, could be helped best in Israel where the MALBEN, an arm of the JDC, had been set up in Israel to care for these unfortunate individuals. There were only about 600 Ashkenazi and sixty-seven Sephardi Jews left in Shanghai in early 1952. In June, 1953, there were only 440 left in Shanghai and less than 600 in Tientsin and Harbin.

Relief and emigration activities in Tientsin and Harbin also came under the control of the Shanghai Council. By this time, the end of June, 1955, there were only 679 Jewish persons left in these two cities, nearly all of them old.

While the Shanghai Jewish School had closed its doors in June 1951 because it no longer had any pupils, religious services were continued until 1956 in the New Synagogue on Hsang Yang Road. In January, 1956, negotiations for the sale of the building were begun with the consent of the Israeli government, to whom the property had been deeded seven years earlier. The money realized from this sale was used for the relief of local Jews. The synagogue was now transferred to the premises of the Shanghai Jewish Center, which now housed all the Jewish organizations in Shanghai. The club had been closed on the last day of 1955 and more than 3,000 books from its library were shipped as a gift to Israel's Ministry for Education and Culture. Other shipments to Israel included also several Torah scrolls which were to be used by new congregations in Israel which had absorbed close to 10,000 arrivals from China.

Slowly, the Jews left the entire area. By June 30, 1958 there remained only eighty-four Jews in Shanghai, thirty-two in Tientsin and 178 in Harbin. The Tientsin Hebrew Association was officially liquidated in January, 1958.

What remained of this once-flourishing community established in 1904, and which had a population of more than 12,000 Jews, was a new cemetery. The old cemetery had been destroyed when the municipal authorities made plans to expand the city. But the graves—a total of 567—were carefully removed in accordance with Jewish religious requirements. While the four Jewish cemeteries in Shanghai were cared for by the Council, the large cemetery in Harbin also faced difficulties. It should be pointed out, however, that this was not a problem for the Jews alone. The officials ordered the removal of all the cemeteries within the city's limits. The fact that there were 3,500 graves in the Jewish cemetery in Harbin offers mute evidence of the once-active Jewish life in that city. Now their removal had become a problem and funds had to be found to provide new resting places for the Jews who had lived in the once-flourishing city of Harbin.

CHAPTER VI

JEWS IN JAPAN

BECAUSE I DO NOT READ JAPANESE, an explanation is in order at
the outset of this chapter on the history of the Jews in the Far
East. All of the Japanese source material utilized by the author
was first translated into English before it was absorbed and
used. Thus, there is always present the possibility of mistrans-
lations or misinterpretations. At the same time, there is a vast
library on Japan, in English, and I have had the benefit of dis-
cussing the subject with various Japanese scholars who cooperated fully in my investigations and studies.

For example, some of the more important works from which
I have drawn are: Linebarger's *Far Eastern Governments and
Politics, China and Japan* (1954); McNair-Lach's *Modern Far
Eastern International Relations* (1955); Michael and Taylor's
The Far East in the Modern World (1956); and Donald Keene's
Living Japan (1959). There are, of course, many other sources,
some of which will be listed and quoted as the narrative con-
tinues.

First, however, one must attempt to understand Japanese
history, the Japanese people, the islands of Japan, to fathom the
situation of the Jews in that country.

Japan is a large group of islands, stretching over a 1000-mile
area off the eastern shores of Asia. They cover an area of 147,611

square miles, therefore making the entire country about the size of the State of California.

The modern Japanese people are believed to be a mixture of various strains. They include the Ainu (an early Caucasian type, limited to the north of Japan) and a Mongol type (from the Asiatic mainland by way of Korea or Sakhalin). Others came from the Malayan area. All these groups combined to make of the Japanese a distant ethnic unit.

The Japanese people have physical vigor, curiosity, a spirit of scientific inquiry, suave formal courtesy and aesthetic appreciation—according to a number of specialists on these people. They imitate well and absorb, with amazing rapidity, the characteristics of alien cultures. They are brave and stoic and martial. They are a proud people and intensely patriotic.

Any attempt to describe contemporary Japan must include one overwhelming fact: that some 90,000,000 people live on these islands and that the Japanese depend upon exports in order to live. Further: modern Japan and its problems cannot be fully understood unless they are viewed through Japan's history of feudalism and its patriarchal clans that ruled the country. In early times, a clan was a group of family units which claimed a common ancestry and worshiped a guardian god. The Yamato clan had established itself as the leading group and exercised a loose authority over the other clans. The Yamato clan claimed that it originated from the Sun Goddess, to whom all other clan deities were subordinate. Thus, the Yamato clan became the Imperial Family in Japan and its legendary origin became the Imperial myth.

Eventually, the paternalistic clan system gave way to the emergence of the family as a special social unit and the individual was subordinated to the family and its head. The Imperial Family stood as the head of the social order and of the State and thus the Imperial Family provided the ideological unity for Japanese feudalism. The Imperial Family and the Emperor remain the central institution of Japan to this very day. The Japanese therefore possess a sense of historic continuity, since the Emperor is the only descendant of a stone age monarch who still holds political office in modern times. But the Emperor is more than a political office holder. He combines religious, cultural, social and political authority in a way which is difficult to analyze.

In spite of the adoption of the new Constitution in 1947, which bases the authority of the Emperor on the will of the people, the Emperor's literal title is still Tenno, which means "Sovereign of Heaven." This title ties him to Japan's first Emperor, Jimmu Tenno, whose 2600th anniversary of assuming his position was marked on February 11, 1940, the "Day of the Founding of the Empire."

Intimately involved with the position of the Imperial Family is Shinto, which means "The Way of the Gods," and which has been described as the indigenous religion of Japan. Interesting analyses of this religion will be found in William K. Bunce's *Religions in Japan* (1955) and in Masaharu's *History of Japanese Religion* (1930). Shinto is a faith without official scriptures, without a founder and with no organized teachings. Nevertheless, it exerts a deep influence on the daily lives of the Japanese. From Bunce's volume, we learn that as a religion Shinto is concerned with a variety of deities, known as Kami, which vary in nature from the spirit of trees, foxes and mountains to deified ancestors, heroes, emperors and a pantheon of heavenly gods. Chief among them is the Sun Goddess, Amaterasu O-Mikami, the Great Sun Kami, who is the mythological ancestress of the Imperial Dynasty. In his history of Japan, Kenzo Akiyama writes, "What the sun is to the universe, so is the Imperial Dynasty to Japan." The spirit of the Sun Goddess is enshrined in the Imperial Grand Sacred Shrine of Ise.

In primitive Shinto, all things, both animate and inanimate, were believed to have souls. Deities were called Kami, which means "above," and implies superiority. The early Japanese applied Kami indiscriminately to any object which was superior, mysterious, powerful or incomprehensible. The one essential for approaching the Kami was purification from any defilement. There was no sense of moral guilt or sin in Shinto. The purification was accomplished by various magical rites, which still provide the basis for the many purification rituals to be found in modern Shinto. Shrines were erected to house the symbolic gateway dividing the sacred from the secular.

While Shintoism was original with the Japanese, the people also came under the influence of Confucianism, Buddhism and Christianity. The ideas of Confucian ethics started to spread in the seventh century. Naturally enough, the Japanese at first accepted those ideas of Confucianism which supported their own Shintoist concepts. Thus they were quick to adopt the Confucian doctrine that the community is more important than the individual. The Japanese also welcomed the five Confucian relationships (ruler and subject; husband and wife; parent and child; elder brother and younger brother; friend and friend) because these concepts extended the idea of the family nation in which the Japanese believed. Other Confucian ideas taught that the Emperor is the fount of benevolent government; that religion, ethics and politics are a single cultural unity and that all men are by nature created unequal.

The ideology of Buddhism took hold in Japan in the twelfth and thirteenth centuries and affected Japanese civilization most profoundly because it taught spiritual values hitherto unknown in the country. Buddhism took a somewhat different form in Japan, for in that land it stressed the doctrine of salvation through faith rather than through knowledge, and substituted for Nirvana the concept of a paradise in which life after death would be continued in a state of bliss. This philosophy of

Gautama (Buddha), in its Japanese modification and application, helped the people to live in spite of the inequalities that existed in feudal and Imperial Japan.

In describing Buddhism, as well as Confucianism and Shintoism, it is hard to formulate precise definitions or to draw clear lines of demarcation. All three faiths, plus Christianity, seemed to exist side by side in Japan. Linebarger states that a true Japanese can be a Shintoist, a Confucianist, a Buddhist or a Christian, at one and the same time. This concept of co-existence and non-exclusiveness of various religious beliefs explains, in part, why there is no evidence in Japan of religious persecution for the sake of religion and faith. The great persecution of the Christian missionary efforts of St. Francis Xavier in 1549, for example, was due to the fear on the part of the Tokugawa rulers, who identified Christianity with the political and military powers in the European nations because Christianity taught allegiance to one God rather than to the State.

A period of 250 years elapsed before the Japanese again allowed the entry of Christian missionaries. Then, during World War II, missionary efforts were once more identified with "foreign imperialism" and were halted. The resurgence of Christian churches after the war has now slowed up considerably.

Jewish Influence

In recent years there has been some Jewish influence in Japan, and this subject has been discussed at length in newspaper articles and by specialists in religion. It may be well, however, to deal with this development in a chronological fashion.

In 1925, a Dr. Chikao Fujisawa, a professor at Nihon University, wrote an article for "Japan and Israel," which was entitled "The Spiritual and the Cultural Affinity of the Japanese and Jewish People." In this essay, he refers to the thesis of a Dr. Kawamorita, who asserts that the first Emperor of Japan was a scion of the House of King David. The historian, Professor Masayuki Kobayashi, whose name will recur throughout this chapter, said to me about this theory: "I am not sure of his doctorate. He was a scholarly journalist but somewhat mystical." This same article cites another scholar, a Dr. Oyabe, who states that the word Mikado—the ancient title of the Japanese Emperor—can be traced back to Gad, one of the lost ten tribes of Israel. Oyabe is reported as having said that the name of the first Mikado Jimmu means Divine Valor and that he had the characteristic traits of the tribe of Gad. He added that "according to the Jewish legendary tradition, Elijah quit Canaan for the East, riding on his chariot and leading a host of Gad and Manasseh knights anxious to preserve intact the purity and genuineness of their original faith of Israel. This momentous event took place about 240 years before the first Tenno Jimmu held the solemn ceremony of his enthronement." Thus, Oyabe theorized, descendants of these distinguished Israelites might have come to settle in Japan by way of China. He offers evidence that there are in Japan such surnames as Cado, Tsuchimikado, Nakamikado, Oimikado and Manasseh.

Other similarities are mentioned, although Oyabe is not too certain of their validity. He tells of the report that the regalia of King Solomon were presumably carried away during the Babylonian invasion of Palestine and that they reappeared among the Imperial treasures of Japan. One of these treasures, the story has it, was the Sacred Mirror which contained a small golden jar from which, when opened by Yuryaku Tenno, white smoke arose. It is held that this white smoke was pulverized rice. This rice, according to Oyabe, is the Manna of the Bible. He informs us that rice is called Mamma in the Japanese vernacular.

Apart from these similarities of a physical nature, Dr. Fujisawa, in his article, claims that there are also spiritual characteristics which Shintoism and Judaism enjoy in common.

Shintoism, like Judaism, has been able to withstand the influx of foreign cultures. Like Judaism, the author states, Shintoism is a national faith which defies any attempt of "frigid dogmatization." He continues: "The Shintoists are highly appreciative of spontaneity, gaiety, happiness, optimism, and harmony and it is for this reason that their earnest desire is to die a natural death like a decayed old tree which falls quickly to the ground. Therefore, the Christian concept of crucifixion is too stupendous and too disconcerting to be fully understood by an average Japanese." It is also believed that the Hebrews, before developing their strict monotheism, were originally polytheistic. Shintoism, too, while it may have begun as "The Way of the Gods," has developed into a monotheistic character.

Moreover, his analysis continues, Shintoism, like Judaism, ultimately hopes for the realization of world peace and universal brotherhood, as evidenced in the concept of "The Whole World Under One Roof." Shintoism, like Judaism, and unlike Christianity, is—in the writer's mind—"loath to sever religion from politics because the spiritual and the material alike are considered as means to the realization of the Holy." Another analogy to Judaism is Shintoism's abstention from proselytizing, although Shintoism does not oppose people joining the faith on its own merits. Finally, Dr. Fujisawa believes that Judaism and Shintoism may have had the same divine source, because Shintoism, too, exalts a specific land, Japan, as the Divine Land, and her people as "God elected."

Although the ideas projected in this essay are provocative and worth discussion, some of my observations on the material contained in this article will have to wait until we make our acquaintance with Bishop Juji Nakada of the Holiness Church movement. In the preface of his book, *God is a Sun and a Shield,* this revivalist church leader, who died in 1939, expresses the hope that his lectures, given at a Bible Institute in June, 1934, will help the racial movement of Christianity. His book was

translated into English in 1941 by Shiro Seto. Its title is taken
from Psalm 84,12: "For the Lord God is a sun and a shield,"
and on the title page there appears the Jewish symbol of the
Star of David and the Japanese symbol of the Rising Sun.

Nakada, as a Japanese Christian, attempts to prove the superiority of the Japanese race (already proven from every other
point of view, the argument runs) through the authority of the
Holy Scriptures. Nakada complains that the Bible and Christianity have been interpreted far too frequently as belonging solely
to Europeans. He believes that one ought to consider the Oriental people in regard to Christianity, for Jesus Christ was a
genuine Asiatic man. He writes, "God intends to brighten the
essence of the Bible using these Asiatic people of the Far East
at the end of the gospel age. Our Holiness Church is, of course,
not an agency of the European church, but a genuine Japanese
church."

Nakada agrees that the Bible was written chiefly for the
Jewish people, but he is thankful that he has found in it symbols which are applicable to the Japanese race. One of these
symbols is the quotation that gave the book its title: "God is a
sun and a shield." He observes that "the mysterious meaning
of this statement was hitherto not revealed in Christian circles,
but has now come out through the fresh spirit of revival." The
mysterious flag symbol of the sun is a hint of Japan's future
mission.

According to Nakada, the Jewish race is symbolized by the
ensign of a shield, made up of two triangles, which earlier had
been the emblem of King David and was now the emblem of
Palestine. It is God's will that these two nations be united after
3,000 years. Kobayashi asserts that while not all of the members
of the Holiness Church completely supported Nakada, many of
his followers did and thus his theories caused a split which continues to this day. Nakada himself was a passionate hot-blooded
revivalist. He had studied in Chicago and had been abroad many

times. Although he was not a theoretical thinker—according to
Kobayashi—he was an attractive man and an eloquent and powerful speaker and made many converts to his church, but because
of his own mercurial temperament, he was unable to organize
a church of a lasting and stable nature.

I quote the following passage to convey not only Nakada's
views of the Jews but of his followers as well:

"The Jewish people is generally said to be a matchless race
in wealth, brains, talent and technique. We perceive how wonderful a race it is, judging from the fact that almost every number one figure in every sphere and era comes out of this race.
This is surely the most Western of Asiatic people. And the
Easternmost Asiatic people is also the number one courageous
nation in the world and famous for winning every battle in
which it has engaged. This is the Japanese race. . . . It was a
Jewish man in New York, Jacob Schiff, who helped Japan with
a foreign loan during the Russo-Japanese War. Besides, there
are also Jewish people who are at present extending Japanese
foreign markets. As they are persecuted by Hitler, they are buy-
ing Japanese goods and planning an anti-German boycott. The
Japanese are not the kind of people to forget kindness to them."
Although his phraseology is awkward, the feeling and meaning
come through in his statement.

In a sweeping statement, Nakada sees Japan as the Helper
from the Sun rising in the East against all the races that per-
secute the Jews. "Japan alone," he says, "has never done the
Jewish people any harm. Therefore, God intends to use this sun-
rising country (Japan) to save the elected (the Jews) and to
give great blessings of the Kingdom of God for a reward. To
this end, all people must convert, become devout believers in
God, and cleanse their sins through receiving the brilliant light
from Jesus Christ, the sum of righteousness."

Nakada believed in the return of Palestine to the people of
Israel as a prerequisite for the coming of the True Messiah. Be-

cause he prayed for the Jews and was in contact with Jews and friends of the Jews, he became a suspicious character in the eyes of the Japanese authorities. They repeatedly checked up on him and reported to the Ministry for Home Affairs and to the Ministry of Foreign Affairs on the "great influence that he exercised upon the Jews residing in the Far East." The police frowned on his collection of money for the purpose of "establishing a fund for the Kingdom of Jewish People." He began to raise funds for this end in 1927 and by September 30, 1933, he had sent abroad some $14,000. The man who received most of the money was a Herman Newmark in London who, according to the Japanese police, was a Jew. But judging from the fact that others, too, got some of this money who were missionaries, it appears that Newmark was a member of an Oriental Missionary Association.

This brief summary of some of the religious and spiritual forces in Japan shows the vast difference between the Oriental and Western religions. In the Orient, religion is a strong ethical force without the apparatus of centralized theological direction. There is place in the Japanese home for individual prayer but no place for communal worship in the Western sense.

Public worship in the Far East is highly individualistic; each person appears in the Temple or Shrine, claps his hands and stands in silent meditation for a few moments. The clergy is not subject to a rigid set of theological rules or characterized by missionary zeal. While Oriental history has had its fair share of civil strife, piracy and robbery, the fact remains that its historical development is almost free from religious intolerance, theological disputation and organized persecution.

Christian dogma and theology therefore found the road towards its acceptance a thorny one. The insular Japanese spirit, while willing to accept outside influences, tried to remold them to fit their own more ancient traditions. There was some acceptance of foreign things, but also a suspicion of them. This suspicion deepened in times of war against the Western nations, who were identified with Christianity, against which Japan had to fight in order to secure her position in Asia.

Arrival of the Jews

Japanese knowledge of Jews and Judaism was scant. Omitting the theories about the arrival of some of the Lost Tribes of Israel in Japan, it is clear that Jews began to come to Japan as early as the ninth century. They also arrived as traders with Portuguese explorers during the fifteenth century and with Dutch traders in the sixteenth century.

When Japan's ports were opened to the West in 1854, thanks to Commodore Perry, Jewish merchants and adventurers arrived at Yokohama and Nagasaki from England, France, Germany, Syria, India and Iraq. The first Jewish tombstone in the International Cemetery in Yokohama dates from 1865. One of the most famous early arrivals was Elias Sassoon, the son of David Sassoon, who opened branch offices of his father's firm in the ports of Yokohama and Nagasaki.

From 1884 onward, we have reports of active Jewish community life in Nagasaki. In that year, Leo Lessner came from Rumania and became the President of the Beth Israel Synagogue. With the aid of the noted Russian-Jewish banker, M. A. Ginsburg, a cemetery plot was bought. By 1904, there were one hundred Jewish families in the port city. They did not always find it easy to carry out their religious obligations. There is in existence a report that a briss (ritual circumcision) was performed on a Jewish infant boy in Shanghai on July 11, 1904, even though the parents were from Nagasaki, five hundred miles away. A Mr. and Mrs. Moses Katz had the briss performed at the home of Mr. and Mrs. D. E. J. Abraham of Shanghai because there was no qualified mohel (circumciser) in Nagasaki. It speaks highly of the deep religious convictions of Mrs. Katz, who traveled

across the sea with an infant in the heat of summer to enter
her child in the household of Israel.

There was a warm religious spirit among the Jews who came
to Nagasaki following the siege of Port Arthur during the Russo-
Japanese War in 1904–1905. Many Jews participated in this conflict and were taken prisoner. This most famous Jewish prisoner
of the time was Joseph Trumpeldor. The valiant Jewish soldier,
whose father also had served in the Czar's armies, was seriously
wounded at Port Arthur. As a result of his injuries, his left arm
was amputated. Although he could have been evacuated, Trumpeldor preferred to fight on with his Russian comrades. When
the fortress finally capitulated, he and his fellow Jewish prisoners, who numbered 500, were incarcerated for a full year in a
Japanese prison camp. During his imprisonment, Trumpeldor was
busy establishing libraries and schools. It was here, too, where
he developed some of his ideas about establishing a Jewish De-
fence Force in Palestine. After his return from prison camp to
his unit in Harbin, Trumpeldor became the first Jew in the Russian army to be honored by the Czar with a reserve commission.

This phase of Trumpeldor's life is scarcely recalled nowa-
days. He is remembered as a Jewish hero of Palestine, who was
killed in action in 1920 in defense of his people. He directed
his fellow Jews when they were attacked by Arabs. He died with
a bullet in his chest, but before he died, he expressed the thought
which has become a byword in Israel, *"Tov lamut b'ad artzenu."*
("It is good to die for one's land.")

The fate of the Jewish prisoners and their treatment by the
Japanese was of deep concern to American Jewry. They peti-
tioned the Japanese Ambassador in Washington, and he assured
them that "special friendship of the highest degree would be
extended to Jewish prisoners."

While it is not likely that Japan's benevolent attitude was
molded by the Jewish poet, Naphtali Herz Imber (the author
of the national anthem of Israel, "Hatikvah"), who dedicated one

of his poems to the Emperor of Japan, the influence of another Jew may have been decisive.

In order to finance its war effort against Czarist Russia, the Imperial Japanese Government dispatched a special financial agent, Baron Korekiyo Takahashi, from New York early in 1904. The Baron was unable to negotiate a loan in New York, so he proceeded to London where he had difficulty in securing a loan of one million British pounds. His mission, however, was eased, after he accidentally met Jacob Schiff, the noted financier, who happened to be in London at the time. Schiff disliked Czarist Russia's treatment of the Jews; he had a keen business sense and a preference for the underdog, in this case, Japan. He was therefore prompted into speedy action. Through his American banking firm, Kuhn, Loeb and Company, Schiff underwrote fifty per cent of three war loans totaling fifty-two million pounds. The other half was underwritten by British interests. A fourth loan, of thirty million pounds, was negotiated jointly by British and German interests and Schiff's own financial interests. This support was followed by additional loans in 1905 and 1912. The Japanese never forgot Jacob Schiff's aid to them. They saw in him a true friend and did not consider it interference when he urged Japan to enter into negotiations with the Russians. These negotiations led to the Portsmouth Peace Treaty, the prime mover of which was President Theodore Roosevelt.

More than any man outside the Japanese government, Schiff knew that Japanese borrowing power had been exhausted and that a peace settlement was in her own best interests. Thus when Mr. and Mrs. Schiff visited Japan in the spring of 1906, all doors were opened to them. The Emperor Meiji himself gave them a private audience and conferred high honors upon them. The warm friendship between Schiff and the Japanese continued. The Schiffs were particularly friendly with Baron Takahashi, whose only daughter, Wakiko, returned with the Schiffs to the United

States and was their guest for nearly three years while she received an education in New York.

Schiff's friendly attitude toward Japan did not, however, prevent him from criticizing Japan when, a few years after the Russo-Japanese War, it appeared that Japan was joining Czarist Russia in exploiting China.

The close association of prominent Jews with leading government and financial circles of Japan proved most valuable in the years of 1917, 1918, 1919 and 1920. It was during these years that the Yokohama Jewish community became the focal point of Jewish life in Japan. Yokohama was one of Japan's principal ports, and had attracted a small number of Jewish traders some two decades earlier. In 1899, an English Jew, Morris Rosla, organized a Jewish Benevolent Society, whose purpose it was to help refugees arriving from Siberia. This society maintained a hostel for refugees whose limited facilities proved insufficient for the large numbers of Jews who arrived in Japan following the Russian revolution and the chaotic conditions in Siberia.

The Mason Mission

In view of this crisis in the Far East, the HIAS decided, late in 1917, to send to Japan its managing director and the chairman of its Foreign Relations Committee, Samuel Mason. This mission, carried out at a time when America's resources were strained in World War I, brought everlasting credit not only to the able Mr. Mason, but to his agency and to all those affiliated with it and cooperating with it.

It was helpful that Jacob Schiff, whose name was extraordinarily popular in Japan, was an important supporter of HIAS. Mr. Mason's correspondence indicates that the letters of introduction from Jacob Schiff which he carried with him made his difficult job considerably easier.

In January, 1918, the approximate time of Mason's arrival in Japan, a serious situation had arisen with hundreds of women and children stranded in Yokohama. They were waiting to join their husbands who had preceded them to the United States. A change of U.S. immigration policy and the interpretation of this change had made it impossible for the consular officials in Yokohama to grant visas to these women and children.

Thus, Mason discovered, these families were stranded, their bridges burned, and return to Russia impossible because it was from Russia that they were trying to escape. Moreover, since their husbands already were in the United States, they were no longer considered the subjects of any other nation. Fortunately, the entire interpretation turned out to be a misunderstanding. The clarification was contained in a State Department letter signed by Frank C. Polk, and addressed to Jacob Schiff (January 21, 1918). And once again, the issuance of visas was left to the judgment of the local U.S. Consul. This raised the hopes of the refugees that they would not have to remain much longer in Japan.

Mason pursued three courses of action to carry out his difficult task. First, he began by separating the healthy from the sick. Many of the refugees, who had been for months in Vladivostok, were half-starved, ragged and diseased. In Yokohama—according to Mason's reports—they were housed in a small building which was woefully inadequate for the needs of the people. There were only 118 cots for 315 persons; there were no toilets. In one group there were trachoma cases, two Jews who had tuberculosis, two with diphtheria, one with typhoid and one who had had an attack of appendicitis. There also was an influenza epidemic and whooping cough. Mason was greatly aided in his work by W. Fleischer, the well-known editor of the *Japan Advertiser*, who also was a friend of Jacob Schiff. On a previous occasion, Schiff had sent Fleischer $3,000 for the local Emigrant Aid Society.

Mason's second objective was to establish HIAS as the Japan-recognized American agency to take care of Jewish refugees from Russia arriving in Japan on their way to rejoin their families in the United States. There was a danger of the Jews being turned back at Tsuruga, the first Japanese port to which they came, because they did not have 400 yen for "show money." The idea was for the HIAS agent to be allowed to file applications with the authorities on behalf of the refugees, so that they might land and wait until they could move on.

In order to win such recognition, Mason utilized the services of T. Miyaoku, one of Japan's most distinguished lawyers and also a friend of Schiff's. Miyaoku, thanks to his contacts and friendship with the Jewish banker, cut through red tape in a comparatively short time. In presenting his petition for recognition to Baron Goto, the Minister for Home Affairs, Mason said that the HIAS represented 89,999 members and 5,000 contributing organizations. It may also have helped when he received the support of Baron Shibusawa, who was one of the richest men in Japan. Mason met the Baron through the good offices of Miyaoku. The Japanese government demonstrated its continuing interest in the refugee problem by sending official representatives to a meeting, sponsored by HIAS and held at Cooper Union in New York City, which concerned itself with relief issues for the refugees.

The third course of action—which was strongly recommended by the American Ambassador in Japan—was for Mason to go to Siberia, Manchuria and Russia, to visit and see the areas from which the refugees came and to attempt to solve some of the problems which sprouted at the points of origin. Ambassador Morris, stationed in Tokyo, realistically foresaw an increase in the flow of refugees from Russia through Japan because of the unstable political situation in the Far East. Mason's trip to Vladivostok and Harbin led to the establishment of HIAS' information bureaus in these cities. These bureaus were helpful to the 3,000 refugees stranded between Manchuria and Japan. In Harbin, the bureau later was developed into a vital aid station.

These bureaus assisted the refugees in contacting their relatives in the United States and held out hope to those still in Siberia that they would still find a road to freedom. Because there was an expectation of an increase in the number of refugees, HIAS opened a special emigration house in Yokohama. Eventually, this house became the responsibility of the local community.

The Jewish community in the Far East remained in danger due to the unsettled conditions in the Far East. The community in Vladivostok, in particular, was in peril. Though there were not many Jews in the city, it was a port town and many refugees came to it first. Power in Vladivostok was wielded by General Semyonoff, who was a notorious anti-Semite. The General received some of his political support from the Japanese army in Siberia. Nevertheless, the Japanese joined the United States in a move to protect the Jews of Vladivostok. Thus, Count Uchida, Japan's Foreign Minister, directed General Yizmura, the Commander-in-Chief of the Japanese troops in Siberia, "not to permit any outrages against the Jews."

The Japanese again displayed a positive attitude on the Jewish question when their delegates came to the disarmament conference held in Washington. Prince Iyesato Tokugawa, one of the chief Japanese delegates, said, "We treat the Jews the same as we do all foreigners. An American Jew is the same American to us as an American Catholic or Protestant."

These statements and actions in behalf of the Jews are all to the credit of the leaders of the Japanese government. However, it should be kept in mind that the Japanese continued to be suspicious of all arrivals from Russia. Because of their scant knowledge of Jews and Judaism, the Japanese associated Russian Communism with all people who spoke the Russian language. Zionism, or the Jewish movement to establish a Jewish homeland in Palestine, also aroused their suspicions. Even though Japan had been one of the first countries in the world to endorse the Balfour Declaration and to ratify the Palestine Mandate, not many Japanese understood the philosophy or purpose of Zionism. Indeed, in our own time, the question of what Zionism is also has aroused great controversy!

Japanese newspapers published fantastic and incredible stories about Zionist meetings held in Yokohama and elsewhere. There was one report that stated that the Jews of Japan had decided to establish a Jewish kingdom in Palestine and already had selected their king! An English Jew had come to Japan on a fund-raising mission. Some Japanese believed that he was the man tapped to be the King of Palestine and they therefore assumed that he was a cousin of King George V of Great Britain.

These stories, minor and trivial in themselves, tell us something of the Japanese lack of knowledge of the Jews and it is not to be wondered that, from time to time, Japanese behavior toward the Jews was puzzling, to say the least.

The years after World War I brought to the Far East the first flurries of anti-Semitic literature. Articles appeared in English, Japanese and German, stressing the "world-wide" activities of the Jews to conquer the world (meaning, of course, the Communist conspiracy). Some of this "research" emanated from Manchuria, thanks to the efforts of the White Russians, who seemed never to give up their anti-Jewish activities.

In 1923, a great disaster, the Kanto earthquake, hit Japan. Life in Yokohama came to an abrupt halt and even the newspaper published by the Jewish community—*The Universal Review*—ceased publication. This earthquake brought to an end the continuing development of the Jewish community of Yokohama and the Jews of the city scattered. Some twenty-five families found refuge in Kobe.

Traders from Iraq and Iran already had established a small colony of Jews in Kobe before World War I. They were later joined by a few Russian merchants who had had the vision to come to Kobe for business ventures. These same Russians were extremely helpful to the refugees who escaped from the Czarist regime and from the Communist administrations during the First World War. Their own small, "unofficial" committee consisted of L. Epstein, N. Gingold, S. Michailovsky, S. Rosentool and J. Subotnik. This enterprising group of men provided food, clothing and shelter to more than 1,000 refugees and their families who were seeking to enter the United States. Meanwhile, the Russian Jews of Kobe maintained contact with other Jewish communities in the Far East, particularly the Jews of Harbin, to whom they sent money for a Passover Relief Fund.

Although they were small in numbers, both the Ashkenazic and the Sephardic Jews maintained their own synagogues in Kobe. On the High Holidays, there was the usual influx of worshippers from Tokyo. One of the Kobe residents was a shochet (ritual slaughterer), and he made it possible for the observant Jews to eat kosher food. Occasionally, however, some ritually prepared meat was imported from Shanghai.

The Influx of Refugees

In time, both Yokohama and Kobe became important again in the annals of the Jews. From July 1940 onward, the great flood of refugees, the enormous influx, started. European ports were shut tight because of World War II and the Trans-Siberian Railroad still operated. The refugees hoped to travel to various parts of the free world from the open Japanese ports. Refugees were met at Manchouli, which was the first border stop within Manchukuo, by a representative of the National Council of Jews in the Far East. The next stop was Harbin. Here, too, the refugees were met by a committee, which assisted the transients and provided them with food, lodging and funds. In earlier years, some of these refugees had lived in Harbin, Mukden,

Dairen, Tientsin and Tsingtao. But beginning in 1940, most of them had proceeded to Kobe and Yokohama where, once more, committees helped the refugees.

Between July, 1940 and October of the same year, the arrivals were, in the main, transients with visas to other lands. Many of them however, had come from Poland and Lithuania with transient visas for Japan and without visas to continue to another land. The Lithuanian Jews had obtained visas from a sympathetic and understanding Japanese consul in Kovno, Lithuania. He managed to get for them the so-called "Curacao" visas. Curacao was a Dutch possession which did not require entry visas. This kindly, generous consul issued thousands of such visas in 1940 in a brief span of time, but only some 2,000 persons who held these visas were willing to undertake a long trip to unknown Japan. Even though these visa-holders were authorized to remain in Japan for no more than seven to ten days, the Japanese officials were very considerate in Kobe and, at the recommendation of the local Jewish community, extended the stays from two to eight months. All told, 4,608 refugees were aided by the local committee, with the help of the JDC, HIAS and a few Polish refugee agencies.

Among the transients were many outstanding intellectuals who had literally gotten on the last trains out of Europe. Reference already has been made to the 300 rabbis and yeshiva students of the Mirer Yeshiva. They came to Kobe in February, 1941 and in August left for Shanghai with some 1,100 other refugees.

There were other Jewish residents, transients and visitors to Japan who contributed to the development of Japan. A few names will suffice to indicate who these people were and what they did.

A Mr. A. Schoyer, an American Jew, lived in Japan in the early 1860's, where he published the *Japanese Express*, one of the first English-language newspapers in the country. Another American

Jew, who settled in Yokohama in 1855, introduced horse-racing
in Japan. There were also Jewish businessmen and traders in
Japan at the turn of the century and in 1903 the Lury family
came to Japan from Siberia to set up business. Robert M. Lury
in 1961 was the president of the Jewish Community Center in
Tokyo. He was succeeded by Walter Citrin.

Mr. Fleischer, the editor of the *Japan Advertiser,* already has
been referred to. Fleischer was well-liked and influential and
was friendly with Joseph C. Grew, the U.S. Ambassador to Japan
from 1932 to 1942. Fleischer was one of the founders of the
Japan-American Society and of the American Club in Tokyo,
both of which were important centers of culture in Japan. He
was active as a member of the Emergency Relief Committee,
which helped Jews who came to Japan after World War I.

Two additional personalities should be mentioned at this
point. The first is Richard Soriano, a Jew from France who lived
in Japan and served as a liaison officer in World War I with a
Japanese naval unit in the Mediterranean and was decorated by
the Japanese for his bravery. The second was Professor Alfred
Regensburger, a German-born Jew who taught physics and
chemistry at the Yokohama Technical College during the 1930's.

The Postwar Era

In describing this particular period, I shall shift my focus
from historical researcher to commentator and participant because of my own experiences in Japan during this era. Because
the events of this period are practically contemporary, I can
indulge in long and detailed descriptions of the day-to-day
changes and developments in Japan. But I would prefer not to
linger on details but to concentrate on the main lines of contemporary events.

It was fortunate that even after the Japanese defeat, the Imperial institution remained intact, although it was modified by

the new Constitution of 1947. The Constitution made "the Emperor the symbol of the state and of the unity of the people, deriving his position from the will of the people with whom resides sovereign power." The Emperor thus provided the continuity necessary for the re-building of the war-ravaged country.

The Diet became the highest instrumentality of the State and was the only law-making body in the country. It was the aim of the Allied Occupation powers to strengthen the democratic basis of the new Japanese government by fostering a strong and independent labor movement, a revised and enlarged group of small businessmen and, finally, an independent land-owning peasantry. There were also some basic reforms in the fields of education and teaching methods, which were designed to develop independence of mind within the student in a system which previously had demanded blind obedience and unquestioning respect for authority.

In addition to these social reforms, steps were soon initiated to get the Japanese economy back to a normal peacetime basis. This became particularly important because of the rising tensions between Soviet Russia and the United States and the consolidation of Communist China on the mainland. America's interest in a stable Japan was made evident at the San Francisco Conference in 1951, at which a peace treaty was signed by forty-nine nations. A mutual security pact was signed between the United States and Japan. On April 28, 1952, Japan officially regained her full sovereignty and the Occupation Forces now became Japan's allies.

The presence of the military forces in Japan, with their proportionate percentage of Jews and Jewish chaplains provided rallying points for the civilian Jews who had survived the war as internees at Karuizawa, a mountain resort near Tokyo, and for those Jews who had come to Japan with the establishment of more normal political and economic conditions.

While these Jews were busy trying to establish themselves,

they also were concerned with Japan's relationship to the newly-created State of Israel. One of the returnees was S. Rosentool, who had lived in Kobe from 1914 to 1928. In 1948 and 1949, Rosentool corresponded with Eliahu Elath, the Israeli Ambassador to the United States, and kept him abreast of the Jewish situation in Japan. In letters to Elath and to Gershon Meron of the Israeli Foreign Office, Rosentool urged that Israel send a trade mission to Japan. But this mission did not take form until 1951. This signaled the beginning of official relations between the two countries and led to the establishment of an Israeli Legation in Tokyo in 1953.

Other early leaders of this Jewish community were H. Wohl and L. Greenberg. But many of the communal activities were hampered by the lack of a suitable building. Eventually, a responsible group under the energetic leadership of A. Ponve, the respected chairman of Kobe's World War II Refugee Committee, purchased a large mansion in one of Tokyo's finest residential areas. After extensive remodeling, the building provided for the religious and social needs of the community. It had a beautiful synagogue and educational facilities plus a library. In addition, it had a fine kitchen, several recreational areas, a garden and a swimming pool. This building is now the Jewish Community Center, and was "designed to provide religious, charitable, cultural and social activities for members and guests and to promote good will and friendship with the Japanese people."

The leaders of the community received sympathetic support from Prince Mikasa, the youngest brother of Emperor Hirohito. Prince Mikasa is an archaeologist and biblical scholar who continues to show great interest in the activities of the Jewish community. According to Kobayashi, the prince served as a military officer during the war and studied European history at Tokyo University. At the time of his graduation, the Jewish Community Center was about to be organized and he elected to give it his support. Prince Mikasa's patronage was also sought by two rival Japanese organizations, the Japan-Israel Association and the Nippon-Israel Friendship League.

The Center is administered by an Executive Board, with A. Ponve as its first President. He served from 1953 to 1957. Robert M. Lury succeeded Ponve. During the first five years of the existence of the Center, remarkable progress was made in welding the community into a cohesive group. The reason for this progress is due to a number of factors. It will be recalled that the Jews in Shanghai had an excellent club of their own. And half of the Jews of Japan had come from Shanghai and felt that they needed a center in Tokyo. The fact that there was a Synagogue on the premises was of utmost importance, and while it had no rabbi until 1958, lay leaders and guest rabbis provided some sort of religious life for the community. In August, 1958, Rabbi L. Jacob came from London to fulfill a three-year contract with the Synagogue, but he resigned in the summer of 1959. Since that time the spiritual leadership has been in the hands of the Religious Committee Chairman, Ralph Kestenbaum, a business executive who is also an ordained Rabbi.

In the absence of a rabbi, the presence of Jews in military service was an important influence in the community. Their religious activities helped stimulate interest in the spiritual life of the community as a whole. They were aided by the National Jewish Welfare Board, the officially-accredited U.S. organization in charge of the religious, welfare and morale program for Jewish service men.

This entire combined effort had a good effect on Jewish life, which was especially evident on Friday nights, when many dignitaries and visitors attended services and social activities in the Tokyo Center. They were all surprised to see a thriving Jewish communal life in such a distant and unexpected location.

Another joint venture of the military and civilian groups was the religious school, attended by some fifty children from the ages of six to twelve. Since 1956, when the school was formally opened, it has graduated many classes.

A study of the membership of the Center indicates that the make-up of the membership included Jews of many social, cultural and religious backgrounds. The great majority were former residents of China and Manchuria and were Russian-speaking Ashkenazic Jews. When they left China and Manchuria, they traveled widely and lived in Israel, the United States, Australia and South America before they gradually drifted back to the Far East. First, however, they had acquired citizenship in one of the countries where they had lived. Other Jews were Sephardic and they had come from the Near East. They were French-speaking Jews. The third group—about one hundred— were American citizens living in Japan and representing American concerns. Some of them had come as members of the U.S. Occupation Forces and had remained in Japan after having established themselves in business or the professions.

All of these Jews ranged in religious outlook from the traditional to Reform. Most of them, particularly those with children, agreed on the need for a positive Jewish educational program. This agreement ultimately resulted in their hiring a teacher-rabbi for a three-year period. The fact that it took more than five years to reach this decision was an indication of the uncertainty and the instability with which some viewed the future of the Jews in Japan.

Another major influence on the life of the community was the establishment in Tokyo, of the Legation of the State of Israel in 1953 and the arrival of its first Minister, Joseph I. Linton. Linton later left Tokyo for a diplomatic assignment in Switzerland in 1957. His successor was Amiel E. Najar, who, in turn, was replaced by Daniel Lewin.

The establishment of the Legation offered additional opportunities for social and cultural events and the presence of diplo-

mats representing the new state of Israel added prestige and
dignity to the occasions. The new state also had a marked influence on the Japanese people and its leaders. Because of the
Legation, there were new opportunities for the Jews to make
contact with groups hitherto alien to them.

First, there were the Japanese students, whose intellectual
curiosity had been aroused by the birth of the new state. They
felt that they would now have a new chance to understand the
Jewish people. This thirst for knowledge, a Japanese characteristic, continues to this day, and Israeli officials are making strenuous efforts to disseminate information about Israel through
radio, television and lectures all over the country.

A second group was a religious mystical unit, which had once
been connected with the Holiness Church, which was led by
Nakada and, after his death, by one of his disciples. This group
was called the Order of Christian Brethren, which had 2,340
members in 1957. They believed in the restoration of Palestine
to the Jews as a prerequisite to the coming of the Second Messiah. They not only believed in it, but also worked for it with
great fervor. The Japan-Israel Association was closely affiliated
with this group. This association claimed to be the successor organization of a "World People's Cultural Association" organized
by Colonel Yasue in Harbin in 1935. The colonel's son, however,
in an interview with this writer, could not confirm that his father
had organized the group. Its aim was to protect the Jews against
the excesses of the Manchukuo and Japanese authorities. A Doctor Morinaka Yokoo, in an article which appeared in a magazine
published only one time by the association, wrote, "The term
'The World People' was used to camouflage the Jewish people
in order to avoid frictions with the Japanese authorities who had
prejudices against Jews." Before World War II, Koichi Kobayashi, was the executive secretary of the association. After the
war, he headed it.

If one were to judge by the magazine he published (the only

issue appeared in April, 1952) the Association had a very ambitious program which was designed to "establish world peace by cooperation, good will and interchange of cultures between the Japanese and Jewish peoples." In order to attain its goals, the association wanted to propagate Israel culture through the establishment of a library; through cooperation of universities and colleges; through lectures, motion pictures and the publication of periodicals; and the development of close ties among the members of the association and the Jewish people in Japan.

Its second aim was to cooperate with the Jews abroad. This was to be accomplished through constant communications with Jewish organizations; through organizing Jewish tours to Japan and to invite to Japan distinguished scholars and leaders in the arts and sciences.

The third objective, which they called "Social Relief Work," was to include relief for orphans and disabled people and to raise funds for social work.

Its final goal was to establish an Israeli cultural center, which would also assist foreigners who wished to invest in Japan.

It is no wonder that such an ambitious program was supported almost at once, in Japan, in the United States and in Israel, by officials and private citizens. The United States army chaplains in Japan, Meyer J. Goldman, Morton Hoffman and Milton Rosen, were glad to be of assistance and they spoke frequently to interested audiences on the meaning of Judaism and the need for a Jewish Cultural Center in Japan. Professor Kobayashi told me, "What kind of assistance they gave, I do not know fully. Based upon my few personal experiences, I can say that these speeches lent themselves, either deliberately or otherwise, to misinterpretations on the part of the Japanese audiences, who were largely composed of 'Christian Brethren'."

The association made contact in economic circles representing both the Japanese government and private industry. It was especially active in 1952 when an Israeli trade mission visited

Japan. In 1955, Koichi Kobayashi visited the United States and made contact with many national organizations and private individuals. The association is still in existence, but internal dissension has hindered its program and it seems to have lost much of its influence.

During 1952 and 1953, the Nippon-Israel Friendship League was particularly active. Captain Inuzuka served as its President. His views on the Jews were outlined in a speech he made in October, 1938, in which he urged that the Japanese use the Jews for the best interests of Japan. This reflected the general feeling of the Japanese authorities. It is now known that in 1941, Inuzuka published some anti-Jewish material under the pen name of Utsunomiya. Professor Kobayashi told me that Inuzuka spread a great deal of anti-Semitism throughout Japan with his articles and speeches. He was one of the most notorious leaders of the "Society for Study of International Politics and Economics." Inuzuka claimed that this literature was written by his wife. To this statement, Kobayashi said, "This claim apparently means that Inuzuka was not responsible. Then what about his many malicious articles?" Professor Kobayashi made reference to Inuzuka's speeches on "The Origin of Red Thought" in 1932 and in articles written through 1937 to 1939 on "Study of the International Secret Power" and on "Studies of the Jews."

It was reported in the press in 1952 that the Nippon-Israel Friendship League had 400 members (Professor Kobayashi said that this figure was exaggerated considering the small attendance at meetings and their general lack of activity) and planned "to construct a Jewish Center in downtown Tokyo to house its office as well as the synagogue currently located in the Headquarters Chapel Center and the Israeli Legation." None of these plans ever materialized.

Thanks to the efforts of leading Japanese, and with the cooperation of local Jewish residents and the Israeli Legation, a society for Japan-Israel friendship was organized on January 20,

1958. Its patron was, and is, Prince Mikasa. The prince is a gracious personality who represents the Emperor at many official functions. When he attended the Passover Seder celebration conducted by the writer in 1957, he brought with him his own skullcap which had been given to him by the Israeli Minister.

The aim of the society is to foster closer ties between Israel and Japan. Since the inception of the organization, trade and cultural relations between the two countries have been progressing satisfactorily. Evidence to this effect is given in a report which appeared in the *London Jewish Observer and Middle East Review* (January 6, 1961). The report quotes Yoshiaharu Takeno, the Japanese Minister to Israel. The Japanese diplomat offered a series of figures to substantiate his belief that there is a great future for Japanese-Israeli trade relations. He stated that in 1959, Japan imported from Israel potash (Israeli pounds 552,000); copper cement (IP 476,000); and phosphates (IP 91,000). This made for a total of IP 1,119,000, which amounts to 0.7 per cent of Israel's total export. The corresponding figure for 1958 amounted to 0.2 per cent. During the first nine months of 1960, Israel's exports to Japan rose to IP 1, 533, 900 or 0.9 per cent of the total exports showing a continuing rise.

With the easing of import restrictions in Japan, Israel will, in the future, be able to add diamonds to her list of export goods. In turn, Israel will import from Japan cattle feed, textile-spinning equipment, cameras, and other optical equipment, as well as machinery and industrial tools. It is also believed that the expansion of the Zim Lines, Israel's shipping fleet, would help strengthen trade between Japan and Israel after Zim would begin sailing from Elath, in Israel's southernmost region.

Quite apart from economic ties, the minister felt that cultural relations also would be cemented. There had been in Israel a most successful exhibition of Japanese prints and posters which had attracted thousands of admiring visitors. This reaction to Japanese art led the diplomat to hope that Japanese literature, which was practically unknown in Israel, would soon be translated and find readers. He held out similar hopes for the Japanese films, which were artistic and colorful.

The report published in the *Jewish Observer* revealed that there were thirteen Japanese graduate students and research fellows at the Hebrew University, the Weizmann Institute and other educational institutions in Israel. Simultaneously, three Israeli students were completing their education in Japan. Moreover, the Israel Philharmonic Orchestra had performed in Japan in 1960 and had made a profound impression on Japanese music lovers. In all, the total picture was bright.

Conversion to Judaism and Emigration to Israel

In the course of the last few years there have been recurring reports and rumors concerning the conversion of thousands of Japanese to Judaism and their projected emigration to Israel. It also was reported, time and again in reputable journals and through news agencies, that there were special Japanese groups which abided by Jewish customs and traditions and were practicing certain forms of Judaism.

It is an intriguing story and it is no wonder that it has captured the imagination of much of the world. The concept of an Oriental people embracing the ancient faith of the Jews is, somehow, magical and holds the imagination. Following the end of the war, Japan, in general, has not retained the enmity of the Americans, which is surprising considering the bitterness engendered by Pearl Harbor. We have flocked to Japanese color movies; we have purchased Japanese cameras and Japanese prints—lovely works of art, indeed—are sold both by our department stores and in our art shops. There is far more animosity directed at Germany than at Japan, and the recurring incidents of anti-Semitism in Germany and the Eichmann trial in Jerusalem continued to remind the American people, and the world at large, of the German atrocities during the war. Japan, on the other hand, has been dealt with far more gently.

Thus, the story of the conversion to Judaism has been accepted in friendly fashion and with a sense of the bizarre.

I have not been able to discover, however, any such groups of Japanese Jews. And I spent three years of my military service in Japan. Practically the only Jews of Japanese descent that I have found have been those Japanese who became Jews upon marrying Jewish women. But even such marriages are extremely rare. And when they happened, they were not entirely new stories for there have been such mixed marriages since the day the Westerners first met Orientals.

Until the end of World War II, such marriages were infrequently entered into, for Japanese society is very insular. It was extraordinarily difficult for a foreigner to win acceptance into a closely-knit Japanese family unit. When there were alliances, they were, in the main, common-law arrangements and were not accepted by the Japanese people or, for that matter, by Westerners, either.

After the war, on the other hand, worship of the Emperor gave way, to an extent, to democratic ideas and the strict authority of the family head loosened somewhat under the many social and political changes brought about by the defeat of the Japanese in the war.

Contact with the Allied Occupation Forces increased the number of mixed marriages. Usually what happened was that a Westerner took an Oriental wife and the girl adopted the faith of her husband. When a girl married a Jew, she turned Jewish, for this step helped her in adjusting to both her husband and his family. The Japanese themselves were by no means taken aback by such action, as they more or less expected the Japanese wife—as part of her duty—to follow her husband and embrace his religion.

Some conversions that took place were more significant than others. They made an impact on the Japanese and especially upon those who believe in the value of missionary activities.

Let us describe the highly-publicized conversion of Dr. Setsuzo Kotsuji. In 1959, at the age of sixty, he was circumcized at the Shaare Zedek Hospital in Jerusalem and became a Jew. He is now named Abraham Kotsuji, and he has written and spoken freely and candidly of his conversion to Judaism. In the 1960 Fall issue of the magazine *Jewish Heritage,* published by the B'nai B'rith, he tells a great deal about himself and his ideas.

He describes himself as a descendant of Shinto priests and as a man who led a Shinto life in Kyoto, the ancient capital of Japan, in his early years. Then, he says, "One day, at the age of thirteen, I happened to stumble on a Bible translated into Japanese in a second-hand bookstore in Kyoto. Until that moment of discovery, I had played and thought like a boy, but once I began to peruse this new book I found myself a thinking individual into whose mind the spirit of God had blown."

He continues his story, "When I came to Leviticus, I clapped my hands and said to myself that this was exactly like the teachings of my ancestral religion—the same mind, the same spirit, but higher than Shintoism in the teachings about the nature of God."

This contact with the Bible, in Japanese, awakened Kotsuji's interest in studying and mastering the Hebrew language, in which the Bible was written. He began to study in a Christian mission school, where he became a Presbyterian. Later, he continued his studies at various Christian colleges in California and received a Doctorate in Semitic Studies from the Pacific School of Religion. By this time, Kotsuji was thirty-three years of age. Up until the outbreak of World War II, he knew and met few

Jews and gave relatively little thought to the Jewish religion, except as an object of study.

In his essay, he tells us about his meetings with Jews during the war and claims that he saved thousands of them from deportation. He states that he prevailed upon the Japanese Government to show tolerance to many of the refugees who were waiting for visas in various Japanese port cities. He describes a harrowing episode he suffered at the hands of the Kempeitai, the Japanese Secret Police (he uses the term Gestapo), who had questioned him one day. He asserts that he might never have returned to his family were it not for a friend's help, a colonel in the Japanese army, who happened to look into the room in which he was being questioned.

His experiences in World War II made him more certain than ever that he wanted to affiliate himself with the Jewish people. Finally, in 1958, he contacted Dr. Israel ben Zeev of the World Union for the Propagation of Judaism, who helped him on his journey to Jerusalem, where he was formally accepted as a member of the Jewish people. It also appears that this Jewish Union, a missionary organization, was behind Kotsuji's plans to establish a Jewish mission in Japan, for Dr. Zeev has said that "the Japanese are ripe for conversion. Eventually they will become Christians or Jews. But as long as Hiroshima is still fresh in their minds, they are not likely to accept Christianity."

I certainly have no quarrel with those who embrace Judaism out of conviction or for its own sake. While I do not subscribe to active missionary activities, I realize that there are some Jews who support it and believe in it. My own point of view, based on my knowledge of Japan and its people, is that the Japanese are not ready to accept Judaism; they are not "ripe" for Judaism.

It is true that the Japanese way of life had been struck a terrible blow when the Empire was defeated in the Second World War. It also is accurate to state that the Japanese are now groping their way toward a new understanding of the world and are attempting to discover a new philosophy of living which combines the best features of the old world and of the new. It is not difficult to understand that many of the hundreds of thousands of Christian Japanese were shocked and disillusioned when the atomic bomb was dropped by a Christian nation upon the Japanese people.

Nevertheless, I do not believe that Japan's problems, social, religious or intellectual, will be solved if they embrace Judaism. The Japanese are an intellectually curious people. What they want and need is information about Judaism as the Mother Religion of Christianity. Perhaps there will be some who will prefer Judaism to Christianity. But missionary activity will be viewed with great suspicion by a nation and a people that never believed in any exclusive or dogmatic creeds.

I believe that Judaism is of permanent and vital importance for the Jew, but I do not believe that the salvation of the non-Jew (and salvation itself is a non-Jewish concept) depends upon his acceptance of the Jewish faith.

As for Kotsuji himself, he has earned an original place in the history of Japanese-Jewish relations, particularly as a scholar of Semitic languages. The very fact that he underwent a painful operation at the age of sixty is evidence of a strong personality and character.

Yet a nagging feeling persists that Kotsuji's conversion somehow was less than genuine. The great amount of publicity he obtained—and sought—implies a degree of opportunism on his part. A religious experience, especially so serious a personal matter as conversion, need not be heavily publicized. And any serious historian would like to know more details concerning Kotsuji's dramatic claims of saving Jews and his own harsh experiences at the hands of the Japanese Gestapo. We should like a few names . . . facts . . . places.

I happen to have some documents which indicate that prior to World War II, Kotsuji was a member of the Special Investigation (Intelligence) Section of the South Manchurian Railway Company. It is common knowledge that this company was a Japanese-controlled instrument of expansion into the mainland of Asia. The Special Investigation Division's members were loyal Japanese dedicated to the expansion policies of the nation. Kotsuji, as a member, must have been one of these loyal Japanese. It is also known that the authorities asked Kotsuji's opinion on the matter of establishing a Jewish court of arbitration in Shanghai. His considered reply was that such a court should not be "officially authorized, but should only be tolerated because its existence would not infringe upon the authority of the Imperial Prestige."

In trying to piece together all of the elements in Kotsuji's checkered background, I wish I could understand the thoughts and actions of this convert to Judaism.

Those who are interested in Jewish missionary efforts may be pleased to learn about the existence of a Mr. Okamoto, a Japanese who has been studying for the Rabbinate at Hebrew Union College in Cincinnati, Ohio. With him is his wife, the former Miss Kyoto Sato. Her family had been one of the principal supporters of Nakada of the Holiness Church. In spite of this, the former Miss Sato was doing all she could to disseminate information on Judaism. Okamoto is due to be graduated from H.U.C. in 1964, thanks to a special Interfaith Fellowship Grant. It is not possible to predict the future, so we do not know whether Okamoto and his wife will return to Japan after his graduation to work among the Japanese and persuade them to convert to Judaism.

The question of Japanese emigration to Israel has been a popular one and there have been conflicting rumors about it. In 1958, the press reported that about 100,000 Japanese were preparing to go to live in Israel. Meanwhile, the World Union circulated a report that it would be easy to convert millions to Judaism if a program of proselytizing were initiated.

Perhaps some of this talk has been stimulated by the over-population of Japan or by Israel's need for skilled workers. Nevertheless, all these reports seem to be no more than wishful thinking on some one's part. It also is clear that as all these statistics and figures are tossed about, one remembers that six million Jews were wiped out during the Hitler era and that Jews constantly are aware of this tragedy. It is therefore perfectly understandable that Jews should wish to help develop Israel and thereby strengthen the entire Jewish people. But I do not think that conversion and the mass movement of Japanese to Israel would resolve these matters.

Professor Masayuki Kobayashi

Throughout this narrative, the reader has been aware, to a greater or lesser degree, of Professor Masayuki Kobayashi. I have been quoting him, referring to him, and stressing his viewpoint on matters of significance. He was the subject of an article written by a noted Far East authority, Professor Hyman Kublin (*Congress Weekly*, October 22, 1956).

Professor Kublin was a Fulbright scholar who spent much time in Japan and who has maintained contacts with Professor Kobayashi over a good many years. Kobayashi, a Professor of History at Tokyo's Waseda University, was born of Christian parents more than fifty years ago. Through his studies of religious and national minorities of Europe, he became interested in Judaism and, in 1940, published a study on *The Jewish Problem During the French Revolution*. This is a work that is deserving of great attention for two reasons. First, it was one of the very few non-biblical studies of the Jews published by a Japanese scholar in his native language. Second, its appearance at the height of Japanese nationalism and increasing anti-Semitism speaks well of the intellectual honesty and moral courage of Kobayashi.

The war years and the bombardment of Tokyo destroyed his home and library. This experience set Kobayashi back in his research in Jewish history. Still, in 1955, ten years after the end of the war, he issued his major study, *The Jewish Policy of Frederick the Great*. But his efforts were not limited to the history of the earlier centuries. He was keenly aware that current Jewish developments were of importance and interest. He translated into Japanese Norman Bentwich's *Israel* and found a publisher for his translation in 1959. Following his work on the Bentwich book, Professor Kobayashi involved himself in translating into Japanese Harry Orlinsky's work *Ancient Israel*.

It must be emphasized that Kobayashi is not a convert to Judaism even though he attended Jewish religious services and activities, including those conducted by me. Kobayashi has impressed me as a shy and gentle man, but upon more familiar acquaintance, he shows himself to be a deep and articulate thinker. He can be sharp in his observations and I have known him to be quite critical of those who approach Judaism from what he considers to be an opportunistic view.

I feel that the best way I can conclude this study of the Jews in Japan and the attitudes of the Japanese toward the Jews, is to report on Professor Kobayashi's own views and opinions. To this end, I submitted to the Japanese scholar a series of questions in 1958, all of which he answered. I am persuaded that the answers to these questions offer a keen insight into the actual situation and that this material adds considerably to one's knowledge of Japan and the Jews in that country.

For the sake of brevity and clarity, I shall reproduce the question and answer form in which this dialogue was originally cast.

Question: What does the educated Japanese know about the Jews as an historical people?

Answer: It is not too much to say that the most highly-educated Japanese have no idea of Jewish history as a continuous and historical development. Some of the Christian scholars, including priests and specialists in ancient history, have greater knowledge, of course, especially on the age of the Old Testament. Even they, however, know almost nothing about Jewish history during these 1,900 years of Jewish existence after the destruction of the Temple in the year 70.

In general, then, even the highly-educated people have only a fragmentary and superficial knowledge of the Jewish people, and we can perceive in them a trace of the prejudice transplanted from Christian or anti-Semitic Europe. According to their impressions, the Jews, for example are:

—the people of the Old Testament (*all* of them clinging even now to a primitive and too rigorous religion, full of laws and commandments).

—the people who killed Jesus Christ.

—the people as symbolized by Shylock and Fagin.

—the people controlling the world economy or dominating British and American capital.

—the people who played a decisive role in the Russian Revolution and are playing a key role in U.S. politics.

—the people who have been hated and persecuted throughout the ages everywhere in the world and the people killed by Hitler.

—the people who produced such great men as Karl Marx, Albert Einstein and others.

—the people who built up the State of Israel and who more recently invaded Egyptian territory.

Question: What does the educated Japanese know about Judaism as a religion?

Answer: Generally speaking, most educated Japanese may be said to be almost ignorant of Judaism. Among the university graduates and those Christians who are highly cultured, a very few have some idea of Judaism, a vague concept of Hebrew monotheism as the starting point or preliminary phase of Christianity. They have not had many opportunities to become aware that there is a large group of men and women who believe in only one God, consider the Old Testament as their Bible and deny Jesus as the Messiah.

Some Christian priests and theologians know a good deal about the Old Testament religion of the Jews. But because of their Christian point of view, they are limited in their understanding of Judaism and they cannot help having a narrow historical approach to Judaism.

A handful of the university professors and teachers of religion know that Judaism is not a mere "fossil," but a great religious and ethical system of values.

Question: What does the Japanese public know about Judaism as a religion?

Answer: The public has no knowledge at all of Judaism. A certain group of men, who have read some absurd books, think they know about Judaism, but as their source of knowledge is ridiculous, so is their knowledge.

Question: What does the general public know about the Jews as an historical people?

Answer: It is ignorant of the Jews, and so there can be no prejudice against them. We do find, however, a few people who have read some nonsensical books about the Jews promoted by anti-Semites or by those who believe in the "common origin of the Japanese and the Jews." Before and during World War II, the anti-Jewish literature was somewhat prevalent, and after the war, we have witnessed the development of groups who believe Jews and Japanese have a common origin.

Question: Who, besides yourself, can be considered to be authorities in Japan on the Hebrew language, history and religion?

Answer: On the Hebrew language, there are nine Christian scholars and one who is not. The non-Christian is Toshihiko Izutsu, who is a linguist and who has specialized in Semitic languages and has translated the Koran into Japanese. The Christian scholars in the Hebrew language are Setsuzo Kotsuji, Senji Tsuru, Toraji Tsukamoto, Kaichi Baba, Junichi Asano, Kiyoshi Ohata, Masao Sekine, Shintaro Hasegawa and Goro Maeda. Professors Kotsuji and Hasegawa can write and speak modern Hebrew. Kotsuji, as a matter of fact, is the author of a Japanese grammar of Hebrew and Hasegawa is now working on a Hebrew-Japanese dictionary.

The specialists on Judaism are also mainly Christians. They are Zenta Watanabe, Junichi Asano, who appears also as a specialist in Hebrew, Yoshishigo Sakon, Shintaro Hasegawa, naturally, Kiyoshi Ohata, Tetsutaro Kinoshita, Toraji Tsukamoto, Goro Maeda and Tetsutaro Ariga. Practically every one of them, except for Ariga, have been studying Biblical Judaism because of their interest in Christianity, although Ohata and Kinoshita have specialized in Talmudical studies. Ariga has translated into Japanese Dr. Leo Baeck's *Das Wesen des Judentums*.

It should be pointed out, by the way, that there is a striking indifference, or lack of knowledge, about the later developments of Judaism, for all of these scholars are interested in the past.

On Jewish history, I may say that the first six names mentioned in connection with specializing in Judaism must also be listed as scholars of ancient Israel or students of Biblical archaeology. Ken Sugawara and Jukichi Oho are professors of European history. Sugawara was the first Japanese to have specialized in Jewish history. I too may be said to have specialized in this area.

I should add that Prince Mikasa is well-known for his interest in archaeology and ancient and modern Jewish history. After World War II, he enrolled as a history student at Tokyo University. One of his teachers is Professor Ohata, who is an authority on the history of Judaism.

Question: Why, and how, did you become interested in Judaism, or in Jewish history?

Answer: The answer to this question is a long story and I hope I can write it one of these days. Meanwhile, Professor Kublin's article may give you some answers.

But in any case, here are the main reasons why I became interested in Judaism as well as Jewish history:

1. I was born and raised in a Christian family.

2. The development of an academic interest in the problems of national or religious minorities.

3. The rise of ultra-nationalism in the 1930's in Japan as well as in Germany, together with the increase of anti-Semitic propaganda.

4. My personal contact with the Jewish people and their religious expressions, which were made possible with the arrival of the allies and, in particular, the American soldiers after World War II.

5. My introduction to the world of Jewish learning.

6. The fact that there still was abroad a distorted and mistaken view of the Jews, their history and their religion.

Question: How can the knowledge of Judaism and the Jews be deepened?

Answer: I dare say that first we must conquer ignorance or mistaken ideas and replace them with accurate and trustworthy knowledge.

There are many ways to do this, but, in my humble opinion, they must include at least such efforts:

1. The publication, through Japanese translations, of good, reliable historical and scholarly volumes which can be used as introductions to Judaism both for the general public and the more advanced public.

2. The organization of a group—let me call it the Society for the Study of Israel in Japan—which would meet regularly for study and other activities.

3. The issuance and distribution by the Society of an annual

bulletin. I should call it, for example, "Isuraeru-Kenkyu," or Studies on Israel, or Jewish Studies in Japan.

4. Making and keeping contact with important organizations and institutions in foreign countries, and making sure that there were available within Japan books, periodicals and other educational materials pertaining to Jewish matters.

Question: In the United States, a number of universities give chairs for Judaism and Jewish subjects are taught in these universities. Do you think this would be possible in Japan?

Answer: It is possible, of course, but it will not be easy. It depends, I imagine, on the circumstances involved and the kind of effort that is put forth. These conditions, at the very least, must be satisfied:

1. The administration or faculty must recognize the significance of establishing special professorships for the teaching of Judaism.

2. The necessary money to sponsor such a chair must be forthcoming.

In view of the lack of money in Japan's universities and the many subjects now being taught, it is difficult to expect the universities to spend money on Jewish subjects. It is, therefore, a matter of someone contributing the money for this purpose. It is, I should like to point out, possible for some teachers in religion or history, to concentrate on Jewish subjects in the name of "special studies." I did this at Waseda University for many years and I still do it.

It is on this note, in a discussion with an outstanding Japanese specialist on Jewish life, that it is fitting to conclude this report on Jewish life in Japan. What the future years will bring forth, nobody knows. But I should like to believe that I have reported accurately, fairly and with some illumination, on the years that have gone by.

BIBLIOGRAPHY

1. *Archives and Libraries*

Japanese Foreign Office, Tokyo.
U.S. State Department, Washington.
YIVO Institute for Jewish Research, New York.
American Jewish Committee, New York.
American Jewish Congress, New York.
American Joint Distribution Committee, New York.
HIAS (Hebrew Immigrant Aid Society) New York.
British Museum, London.
Kogan Papers: a collection of Japanese papers dealing with Japanese policy towards Jews before and during World War II. They are held by Mr. M. Kogan, Tokyo.

2. *Published material* (listed in the order of their appearance):

Finn, James: *The Jews in China,* London, 1843.
Cordier, Henri: *Les Juifs en Chine,* Paris, 1891.
Perlmann, S. M.: *History of the Jews in China,* London, 1913.
Kawakami, K. K.: *What Japan Thinks,* New York, 1921.
Ezra, E. J.: *Chinese Jews,* Shanghai, 1926.
Wilder, H. E.: *Social Currents in Japan,* Chicago, 1927.
Bloch, J.: *Jewish Life in Oriental Countries,* New York, 1927.
Buechler, A.: "The Jews of Hongkong," *B'nai Brith Monthly,* Washington, November, 1931.

Young, C. Walter: *Japan's Special Position in Manchuria*, Oxford, 1931.

Brod, Max: *Abenteuer in Japan*, Amsterdam, 1938.

Vespa, Amleto: *Secret Agent of Japan*, London, 1938.

Weinberger, J.: *Central Management of the I.C.R. Homes*, Shanghai, 1939.

Reiss, Felix: "Report of the Medical Board," Shanghai, 1940.

Barnett, Robert W.: *Economic Shanghai, Hostage to Politics 1937–41*, New York, 1941.

Postal, Bernard: "The Jews in China," Universal Jewish Encyclopedia, Vol. 3, New York, 1941.

Margolis, Laura L.: "Race Against Time in Shanghai," *Survey Graphic*, New York, 1944.

Shanghai Herald: Special Newspaper edition, Shanghai, 1946.

Shanghai Almanac: edited by O. Lewin, Shanghai, 1947.

Buck, Pearl S.: *Peony*, New York, 1948.

Hinzelmann, Hans H.: *Oh China, Land auf alten Wegen*, Braunschweig, 1948.

Strauss, Ernest: "The Far East," *American Jewish Yearbook*, Vol. 50, Philadelphia, 1949.

Sassoon, D. S.: *A History of the Jews in Baghdad*, Letchworth, England, 1949.

Jones, F. C.: *Manchuria Since 1931*, London, 1949.

Sjakovsky, S.: *Catalogue, Exhibition of Jewish Life in Shanghai*, YIVO, New York, 1950.

Gruenberger, Felix: "The Jewish Refugees in Shanghai," *Jewish Social Studies*, New York, 1950.

Reischauer, E. O.: *The United States and Japan*, Cambridge, 1950.

Schwarz, S. M.: *The Jews in the Soviet Union*, Syracuse, 1951.

Murphey, Rhoads: *Shanghai, Key to Modern China*, Cambridge, 1953.

Finch, Percy: *Shanghai and Beyond*, New York, 1953.

Jones, F. C.: *Japan's New Order in East Asia, Its Rise and Fall 1937–45*, Oxford, 1954.

Linebarger, P. M. A., Djang Chu and Burks, A. W.: *Far Eastern Governments: China and Japan*, New York, 1954.

Bunce, William K.: *Religions in Japan*, Charles E. Tuttle Co., Rutland, Vt., 1955.

Stoetsel, Jean: *Without the Chrysanthemum and the Sword*, New York, 1955.

Michael, F. H. and Taylor, G. E.: *The Far East in the Modern World*, New York, 1956.

Rabinovitch, S.: "The Jewish Settlement in China," *Gesher*, Hebrew Quarterly, Israel, 1957.

Roth, Cecil: "The Past, Present and Future of the Sephardim," *Le Judaisme Sephardi*, London, 1957.

Shigemitsu, Mamoru: *Japan and Her Destiny, My Struggle for Peace*, New York, 1958.

Callis, Helmut G.: *China, Confucian and Communist*, New York, 1959.

Keene, Donald: *Living Japan*, New York, 1959.

3. *Unpublished Material:*

Rosenfeld, M.: *History of Jews in Shanghai*, written in 1944, YIVO Archives, New York.

Kranzler, D.: *The Shanghai Jewish Community*, Dissertation, Brooklyn College, 1958.

INDEX

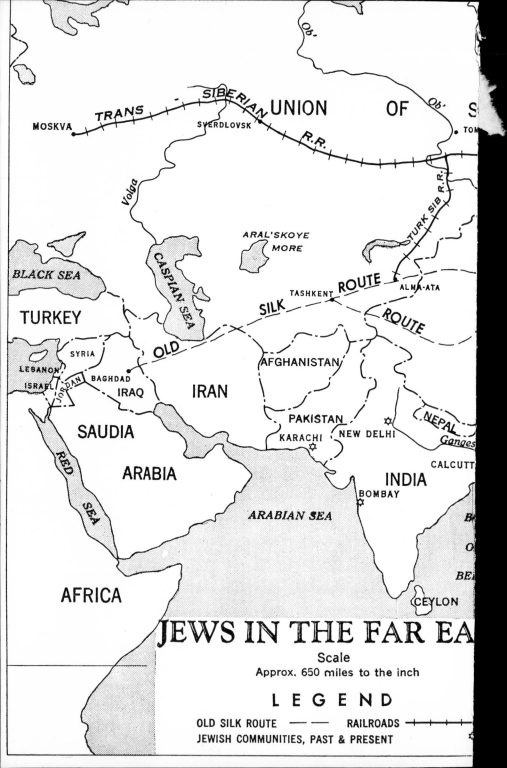

JEWS IN THE FAR EA[ST]

Scale
Approx. 650 miles to the inch

LEGEND

OLD SILK ROUTE — — RAILROADS ┼┼┼┼

JEWISH COMMUNITIES, PAST & PRESENT